After his _____ Seed, a friar priest of the Franciscan order, went ___ to achieve three university degrees and two doctorates, and has served ___ Westminster Cathedral for ___ Ecumenical Affairs under the late Cardinal Basil Hume and Cardinal Cormac Murphy-O'Connor.

Known as the priest to the stars, he is an established and familiar figure in Parliament and a regular visitor to Downing Street, having been on friendly terms with the last six Prime Ministers. He is also equally at home in the Vatican, the City, Buckingham Palace and in the world of show business, and is a leading supporter of many charities, including The Passage, the London centre for the homeless.

His conversion to Catholicism of Anne Widdecombe, John Gummer and the outrageous Alan Clark made him the celebrity priest of the century, according to *The Times*.

In 2004 Pope John Paul II awarded him the highest Vatican award – the gold cross Pro Ecclesia et Pontificia – for his contribution to international ecumenical and inter-faith affairs.

He is also a well known speaker, newspaper columnist and author of several books.

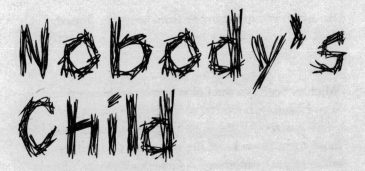

Nobody's Child

Michael Seed

with Noel Botham

metro

Published by John Blake Publishing Ltd,
3 Bramber Court, 2 Bramber Road,
London W14 9PB, England

www.johnblakepublishing.co.uk

First published in paperback in 2008

ISBN: 978-1-84454-588-9

British Library Cataloguing-in-Publication Data:

A catalogue record for this book is available from the British Library.

Design by www.envydesign.co.uk

Printed in Great Britain by CPI Bookmarque, Croydon, CR0 4TD

3 5 7 9 10 8 6 4

Papers used by John Blake Publishing are natural, recyclable products made
from wood grown in sustainable forests. The manufacturing processes
conform to the environmental regulations of the country of origin.

Every attempt has been made to contact the relevant copyright-holders, but
some were unobtainable. We would be grateful if the appropriate people
could contact us.

This book is dedicated to my grandmother,
Mary Ramsden, and Cardinal Basil Hume O.S.B., O.M..
I also wish to remember those beloved people who have
given me a part in their lives these past fifty years.

Friends of Michael Seed

Martina Cole, Novelist

I have known Michael for a good number of years now, and he never ceases to amaze me. My son, Chris, is also a friend, and on many occasions we have all shared a drink, and humorous stories together, over meals in our favourite Soho restaurants.

He's a great friend if one is needed, and a good listener, with a compassion and fair mindedness that puts most people to shame.

He's also a wonderful priest and very good company. Michael, as my old mum used to say, could make a cat laugh. He has a great humour that brings to his story the human element which is missing from so many other tragic biographies.

His love for his mother, and his belief that somewhere, and at some time, a life would eventually beckon which would help him overcome all the ills that had befallen him, made me feel a new vigour for my own life and troubles.

I read this manuscript with some trepidation, because after all, this was the awful story of his private life, talking about things he had previously only hinted at in our conversations.

However, after sitting mesmerised for half the night, my feelings were mainly of deep sorrow, and a deeper sadness that someone's life should be so blighted by the very people who were supposed to love him, cherish him and mature him.

My most overwhelming emotion though, was one of complete and utter admiration, for a man who could overcome such an upbringing, and instead of using it as an excuse for the sorry state of his life, could overcome it, to such an extent, and make other people's lives better. Michael can reach inside himself, and take his own experiences and use them to understand the plight of others.

This book is not an easy read, but it has one thing so many of these tragic biographies often lack. There is no self pity and no '*Oh why me?*'

Rather he seems to have accepted it all as part of a greater plan.

Read this story and weep, knowing that every word is true, but expect, as I did to feel a connection with this sad child, who knew, deep in his heart, there was something better waiting for him, and who ultimately found it by giving himself over to a higher authority, and by dedicating his life to people less fortunate than himself.

Michael is a lovely man and a wonderful friend. He is kindness itself, and has a gentleness that brings out the best in people.

I hope you read this and feel a difference in your own life, as I did in mine. Because no matter what happens to him he finds a way to overcome it and make some good come out of it. That's something we can all understand at some time in our own lives

Lord Jeffrey Archer

Father Michael Seed is a rare and remarkable man, whose life story is far more incredible than any best-selling novel.

Michael mixes with prime ministers and ordinary folk and treats us all with the same kindness, warmth and wisdom that have won him so many friends from all walks of life.

His story is an inspiration to us all, and in particular for anyone who feels life has been hard on them, for Michael has overcome obstacles that would have put off a battle-hardened marine let alone a normal mortal.

But, above all, what shines through in this book is

Michael's faith which has sustained him through so many troubles on a journey that will keep you turning the pages, and in the end you can only wonder what else is in store for this man who can best be described as the Good Samaritan.

The Right Honourable Ann Widdecombe MP

Michael Seed was the priest who converted me to Catholicism and received me into the Church in the midst of a media circus which turned the normally quiet, dignified Westminster Cathedral into a veritable bedlam. Life was not the same for either of us thereafter.

In the 20 years since we first met, I have got to know Michael well, not only as a priest but also as a close friend. He is humorous, kind and a very dedicated friar but, from time to time, he has dropped hints of a time when life was bleak and those of us who know him know also that his childhood was scarred by a suicide. Nothing could have prepared me for the real story which is truly scandalous in the number of adults who passed by on the other side while an innocent child fell victim to bullies and perverts.

That Michael emerged clever, sensitive, kind and sane is a genuine miracle and we should all thank God for this man's resurrection from hell. Read on and wonder...

Foreword by Michael Seed

A large part of me felt that this book should never have seen the light of day. There is no one to blame but myself. Finally, after years of discussion with my good friend, publisher John Blake, it is over. Am I happy? I don't know. Close friends tell me it will help others – a glimmer of consolation. This book is very basic and brutal and I hate its content myself. I can only apologise to those who might now see me in a different light.

I wish to record my deepest thanks to my dear friend of nearly twenty years, Noel Botham, without whose dedicated help this book would not have been possible.

If you read my book you will no longer be surprised I needed assistance in its writing. My problem in committing anything to paper has been a continuing, and emotionally disabling one. Even today, all my sermons and lectures are planned mentally, and remembered. I can give an hour-long talk without even referring to notes – there are no notes. Nature appears to have compensated for my severe dyslexia and difficulties with written communication by blessing me with an exceptional memory.

In the past Noel has helped me with two books to raise funds for The Passage, the charity for the homeless founded by the late Cardinal Basil Hume. It seemed only natural, when I agreed to tell my story, that I should again seek his help.

I trusted him to transfer my spoken word to the pages of this book as far as is humanly possible, and he has done a remarkable job, even down to capturing my emotional reaction to fully reliving it for the first time.

I would also like to thank John Blake and his wonderful team for their sensitive handling of the book and its publication.

Prologue

Our family lived in one of Manchester's worst slums, a neighbourhood long condemned by the council and gradually being demolished around us, street by street, house by house.

My earliest memories are of Mammy and me wanting to escape. Not from the squalor of life in Openshaw, but from the terror and the hatred and the violence. From the man who beat and tortured us: my daddy. The best we managed together was to steal away in the afternoons with a friend of Mammy's. They were the only happy moments I remember from my childhood.

I did try to run away alone once – to live with the gypsies – but I was found and dragged home and beaten unconscious by Daddy. I was too terrified to ever try again.

But Mammy tried to escape many times – and, finally, when I was eight years old, she succeeded. She threw herself in front of a train and left me to cope with life and Daddy without her.

After that, every day for five years I thought of trying to follow her by killing myself. I even lay on the track, in the exact spot where she had died, hoping to die under the wheels of the same train. But, each time, at the last moment, something more powerful than my desire to die made me scramble to safety.

Sometimes today I still cry for the lonely, frightened little boy I was then – so unhappy and so longing for love – and marvel at not only surviving the brutality and the other appalling abuse but also, in the end, triumphing over it all.

As that boy, I found it difficult to understand when other children talked of having nightmares in their sleep. For me, sleep was the only time when I felt truly safe.

The nightmares I dreaded were always waiting for me when I awoke.

Contents

PART ONE

Chapter One

I can't remember a time when Mammy and Daddy didn't shout at each other and when he didn't hurt us. The arguments and the pain were a part of our family life and I thought they were normal. Shouting and snarling and lashing out, Daddy would always win. Sometimes Mammy would shout back, but most of the time she just stood there, as though in a trance, and did not even answer him.

There were always slaps. On the legs and bottom and arms – and occasionally across my face. And slaps for Mammy too. But sometimes he would punch her in the face and her lip would split or her eye blacken, and she would scream louder than usual. Then we would cling to each other, huddled on the floor behind the settee, while she sobbed and I gritted my teeth, determined not to cry like a baby, and we would wait until Daddy had gone out or gone to bed.

Then Mammy would crawl on to the settee and go to sleep. The settee was where I was supposed to sleep, but on those nights I would collect the old blue-and-white baby blanket my nanny had crocheted for me and a pillow, and make my bed on the floor in the corner. Sometimes Mammy had already taken my blanket and I would curl up in one of the easy chairs to try to keep warm. But they were covered in shiny, cold, black plastic and provided little comfort.

We had no central heating and the fire, which was wide and deep and had cast-iron ovens on either side that were never used for cooking, was always allowed to die down at night – even in the middle of winter – so sometimes it would be freezing cold. To me, it seemed I often spent the whole night shivering, and in the morning the inside of the window would be covered in frost, which would gradually melt as the fire warmed the living room. That is, if Mammy had remembered to fetch coal and actually restarted the fire. On those days, I would wait until she had gone downstairs, then rescue my blanket and stay huddled up in a chair to keep warm.

At the time, I thought very little about the cause of all this violence and misery – I was far more concerned with the very real and painful effect it was having on me – but later I was able to piece together my parents' story.

My mother's name was Lillian and, as a young teenager, she was acknowledged to be the prettiest girl on the council estate where she lived in Bolton. Her parents were in the Salvation Army and she was being groomed to become an officer in the movement. My grandmother, Mary Ramsden, who was known to everyone as Polly, told me that Mammy was then in love with a young Salvation Army officer, Harold, who would later become one of the movement's top officials. She would have loved Harold to become her son-in-law and always hoped they would marry.

But, during the war, Mammy met Joe, an RAF navigator, and fell in love with him. Joe, who was to become my father, was a Roman Catholic whose parents were a well-to-do couple from Liverpool.

This, Nanny Ramsden later told me, was the start of their problems. For Joe's parents believed he was marrying beneath him and, even though Mammy converted to Catholicism, they remained bitterly opposed to the marriage. Daddy's mother, Florence, even threatened to kill herself if the marriage went ahead.

But it did, and she, I would very much regret later, didn't. The wedding took place in Bolton in 1942. According to family gossip, the Ramsdens and the Seeds did not exchange a single word on that day – or afterwards.

Twenty years later, in our house in Manchester, all the poison and the forecasts of disaster which had shrouded their marriage had festered and grown and were now tearing our family apart.

Even had I understood the cause of their conflict – and I was never really certain what it was – I had no way of preventing what was happening. I was only four and unable to defend or retaliate. Half the time Mammy didn't seem to know I was there and to Daddy I was just 'a good for nothing', 'a bad boy', 'a useless brat', 'a waste of space'. I was, he frequently told me, 'nobody's child'. And I believed him. I grew up accepting that I was bad and stupid, but also that our family was no different from any other. This, I thought, was the way all little children and their mammies were treated.

Ours was a small two-storey terraced house, number 447, the corner one of a long row of identical properties with smoke-blackened bricks and dark slate roofs. The front doors all opened directly on to a wide pavement and were faced, across the busy Ashton Old Road, by a row of identical houses.

I didn't know then that we were right in the centre of the square mile or so of the most deprived part of Manchester. The houses had yards at the back and little lanes separating them from more identical houses behind them. Car-repair shops and other light-engineering businesses were run out of lock-up garages in the yards along these lanes.

There were already gaps between some of the houses where buildings had been wiped out by German bombs during the war. The council had put up advertising hoardings, promoting products like Oxo and Persil, to fill the spaces where once there were homes. There had been no attempt to rebuild because the whole dump was scheduled for demolition and redevelopment.

Compared with our neighbourhood, Coronation Street looked like Millionaires' Row. There were always lots of people and noise, and most families seemed to have three or four or more children. I think I was the only lone child in our street.

Where the downstairs rooms were in the other houses, ours had been converted into a shop, run by my mother, that sold sweets, cigarettes, fizzy drinks and sandwiches. Most of the local women would pop in to buy stuff and to gossip.

My mother was very beautiful and everyone liked her. The only person I ever knew who didn't like her, apart from Daddy's mother, who hated her, was my father himself, and I was always puzzled as to why they had chosen each other when they so obviously couldn't get along.

We lived on the first floor, which had a big living room at the front, a bedroom at the back and a tiny kitchen and toilet in the middle. There was no bathroom. We took our baths in a galvanised tin tub in front of the fire once a week. Except Daddy, who said he showered at work.

The place smelled permanently of damp and was always dirty. In the living room there were stained and grimy floorboards on which lay three small, cheap and badly soiled machine-made rugs. The wallpaper, plain white and unpainted and covered in damp marks and stains, was peeling away from the walls in places.

On the floor of the small kitchen was brown linoleum, cracked and worn through in front of the sink. Nothing was ever polished and the windows were only ever cleaned by the rain. I rarely saw Mammy use a brush around the place, but she was fastidiously clean when it came to her personal hygiene, strip-washing in front of the sink every day.

Ours was a slum dwelling in a slum area and we lived in appalling conditions, but I didn't realise then that we were very poor. There was very little furniture. In the living room, there was only the settee and two easy chairs covered in shiny black plastic, which was torn in places and crudely fastened together with sticky tape, a small table and three kitchen chairs and a radio. When I was nearly five, Daddy bought a second-hand, black-and-white TV with a tiny 12-inch screen.

There were no family meals in our house. I would sometimes eat at the table in the living room, but I can't remember the three of us ever sitting down together to eat. My mother never actually prepared a meal for me. Sometimes there would be a packet of cereal in the kitchen and I would have to go downstairs to the shop to fetch milk. Unless there had already been a delivery that morning, it was often warm and not very nice.

One day, when I was four, I went down and grabbed a bottle of milk that turned out to be completely sour and curdled. It made me very sick and I have never drunk milk on its own since then; occasionally in tea or coffee, but never alone. But already I had learned that complaining made no difference. It was not, I think, because Mammy didn't care. She just didn't seem to know I was there. Most days, it was just as though I was invisible. Her eyes would be open but she didn't seem to see me or hear me.

From overhearing neighbours' gossip, I knew that Mammy suffered from something called 'depression' and that she was taking lots of very strong tablets called 'anti-depressants' and 'tranquillisers'. These had a very odd effect and she would go for long periods as though she wasn't really there.

When this happened, I would tell myself that Mammy was switched off. She wasn't working properly. And I knew not to pester her with questions, because I knew also that I would either get no reply at all, or mixed-up answers that most of the time didn't make any sense at all.

Often it was just like having a beautiful, big, walking doll in the house. She moved around but you couldn't speak to her.

I stopped telling Mammy that there was nothing to eat when I was about four, because usually all she would do, if she acknowledged me at all, was point vaguely down in the direction of the shop.

Occasionally, a new box of cereal would appear in the kitchen and I assumed she had been shopping. But there was no pattern to this and sometimes for weeks on end there would be nothing upstairs for me to eat. More often than not a banana or an apple would be my breakfast – and dinner too.

Mammy never prepared an evening meal for Daddy either – and that was the cause of many of their rows. I learned much later on that, in the early years of their marriage, when romance was still alive, she used to cook meals for him like any other wife. But 15 years of a brutal marriage and the eventual onset of serious clinical depression had dramatically altered that. By the time I became aware of what was going on, she had stopped cooking for Daddy entirely.

At lunchtime, there was a set routine. I would go down to the shop and be given a sandwich. Mammy made sandwiches, using the cheapest sliced bread, behind the counter for the local workmen, and, as a small boy before I started school, I survived mainly on a daily diet of cheese and pickle or ham and tomato sandwiches and odds and ends of fruit.

I came to hate the taste of cheese and ham but I would force myself to swallow them down rather than go to bed hungry. By then, I knew that there was very little chance of getting anything substantial to eat before I went to bed. And I was only too aware of the hunger pains that accompanied a rumbling, empty tummy while waiting for sleep to come.

Luckily for me, we were surrounded by good neighbours, and I'm sure most of them must have been aware of my mother's haphazard catering arrangements for her family. I don't think any of them were better off than us – most of their homes were just as sparsely and shabbily furnished as ours, and they had more hungry mouths to feed – but the local mums nearly always offered me some titbit or other when I went round to play with their children. I could usually count on being given a currant bun or a slice of home-baked cake or some other treat to supplement my meagre home diet, and told, 'Come on then, love, tuck in now.' Usually this was accompanied by a pat on the head and a comment like 'poor little mite' or 'poor bairn'.

At the time, I couldn't understand why I was such a poor creature but I welcomed the food and all the impromptu hugs the other mums gave me. Hugs were something to cherish. I never got them at home. Mammy never cuddled me or kissed me. I think she only ever held me for her own comfort when she was frightened or hurt. And the only times then that Daddy ever touched me was when he lashed out in anger.

During the day, I used to spend hours alone in the living room watching television. Mammy never seemed to care what I did or what I watched, and in fact most of the time I don't think she even knew where I was. After a while, it became obvious to me that the families on television were all very different from mine. The mothers all seemed to be happy and smiling and spent lots of time playing and talking with their children, and cleaning their homes, and the fathers nearly always seemed pleased to see them. The dads took their children out to play ball games in the park.

I asked Mammy one day, 'Why doesn't Daddy like us?'

It happened to be one of her more communicative days and she told me, 'He loves us really. He just gets very angry and can't help himself. It's the devil in him, mixed with the drink.'

I didn't know much about the devil but I reckoned, if that was who was making Daddy beat us, he wasn't very nice.

I also knew that if Daddy came home smelling of beer — a smell I knew from when he drank bottles of the stuff in the living room — he was more likely to start shouting and hitting out than at other times. If I caught an early-warning smell of beer on his breath, I would either run out to play in the yard or sit down very quietly behind the settee.

Anything, however small, could trigger an explosion, but one of the things which often made him angry was the way Mammy dressed, and the make-up she wore. She was very pretty and people said she didn't need to wear the amount of mascara, powder and lipstick she sometimes used. She liked her skirts just above the knee and most of her blouses and dresses were low-cut at the top and showed a lot of her breasts. She also loved cheap imitation jewellery.

Mammy said that how she dressed was one of the few ways she had of brightening her life. Daddy said she tarted herself up like a slut and beat her because of it.

Chapter Two

Daddy was a warder at the notorious Strangeways Prison in Manchester, and in uniform he always looked a bit scary, not just to me but to the other kids in the neighbourhood too. Some of those kids would be cheeky to almost anybody. But not to my father. Perhaps they had heard stories about the beatings he gave Mammy and me, but they seemed to know not to mess with him.

His black uniform jacket and trousers were like a policeman's and were complemented by a shiny, black peaked cap, white shirt and black tie. Daddy always kept his hair very short at the back and sides, which helped to make him look very fierce. At that time, he always seemed to be angry about something and I don't remember ever seeing him smile.

He carried a whistle, which he once let me blow, and a black baton, and wore a thick, black leather belt with a large buckle. He was a tall man and quite slim, though his arms were hard with muscle. Daddy often told me he was the fittest and toughest man at Strangeways, including the prisoners, and that he was a match for any of them.

I don't know if that was true because, apart from a crazy situation when I was older, I only ever saw him hit Mammy and me – and neither of us could put up much of a fight.

The first beating that was different, and I can still remember it vividly, was when he made me bleed for the first time and dragged Mammy into the bedroom to do things to her. As usually happened, she was half-asleep in an easy chair when he came in, and I was watching *Dixon of Dock Green* on television. I heard Daddy's footsteps coming up the stairs and I shuffled myself as far back into my chair as I could, trying to make myself less noticeable. I had long since learned that out of sight meant out of mind and that I was less likely to receive a slap if he didn't notice me.

Mammy didn't look up when he came in. Perhaps she didn't even know he was there. That often seemed to be the case with her. Her eyes could be open but she didn't appear to see what was happening around her.

Daddy marched over, still wearing his cap, and stood, legs apart, in front of her, just staring down. Then he reached down and shook her by the shoulders. 'Can't you ever be bloody normal when I come home?' he shouted. 'Well, don't think you can get out of your duties by doping yourself into stupidity, 'cos you can't. You're like a bloody zombie. Absolutely useless. It's like being married to a corpse.'

Mammy seemed to understand something and tried to push him away. 'Stop it,' she said in the sort of sing-song voice she sometimes used. 'I don't want you to touch me. You hurt me.'

'I'm not hurting you,' he yelled, his face only a few inches from hers, 'but if you like I'll give you something to hurt you,' and he slapped her hard across the side of her face with his right hand.

Mammy screamed and I jumped from my chair and rushed over to him. He was still leaning over her and I grabbed hold of his sleeve and pleaded with him. 'Please, Daddy, don't hit Mammy any more. You're hurting her.'

'What the hell do you want, you stupid boy?' he snarled. 'And what are you doing here anyway? You're nobody's child. Don't you understand that, you little brat? You're nobody's child.' He glared at me, then undid his belt buckle and began to take off his belt.

'Please don't hurt us,' I said again, but it was far too late for that.

He pulled his belt free of his trousers, folded it in half lengthwise and suddenly swung it violently at my legs.

The pain was awful and I couldn't help screaming. 'Please don't, Daddy,' I yelled again.

But he was too angry to listen and he lashed at me again. This time the belt landed across my shoulders and the buckle end wrapped around my head and smashed into my face.

I screamed again and put my hand up to my face. I was in agony. I felt my face was wet and thought it must be tears, but when I took my hand away it was red with blood. The big metal buckle had split my cheek.

Daddy was already raising his arm for another blow, but when he saw the blood he paused with his arm in the air.

Mammy was still crying – but not for me. Although she was staring towards me, I don't think she knew what was happening. Usually, if she wasn't drugged, she would try to stop him when he started beating me. But this time Daddy seemed to think I had had enough.

'Stop your bloody snivelling, boy, and go and wipe your face,' he said, and returned his attention to Mammy.

'Please don't hit her again,' I pleaded.

'Just do as you're bloody told, you stupid brat,' he shouted. 'I want my dues. She's going to do her damned duty one way or another, or I'll wring her bloody neck.'

Then he reached down and pulled Mammy to her feet by her shoulders. She tried to sit down again and he hit her across the face again. With a scream, she dropped to her knees in front of him. Her lovely face was now all red and blotchy and she was crying.

I thought then that he was going to punch Mammy,

but I was just too terrified of what he might do to me to try to help her.

Instead, he grabbed her by one arm and the scruff of her neck and dragged her, her heels scraping across the floor, out of the living room, cursing her all the way.

'Now we'll see who's the master here,' he yelled and hauled her into the bedroom and slammed the door.

I found a dirty teacloth in the kitchen and held it to my cheek, which was still bleeding and really smarting. I crept into Mammy's armchair and curled up into a ball. *Dixon of Dock Green* was still on, but it wasn't loud enough to drown out the sounds of Mammy's cries and Daddy's curses.

I don't know what he was doing to her to hurt her, but I wasn't big enough or strong enough to help. And I was too frightened anyway.

Eventually, I must have gone to sleep because the next thing I remember it was daylight and the television was fuzzy and making a funny high-pitched noise. From the bedroom there was not a sound.

Chapter Three

Whether Daddy had stayed the night or gone to work early I didn't know, but that morning Mammy must have forgotten to take her pills because she was talking and acting quite normally.

I thought that perhaps something had happened with Daddy the previous night which had changed her, but it didn't really matter. I was just so pleased to have her with me once again after such a long time. The real Mammy, not the half-asleep person who looked right through me.

I didn't dare to hope that the change would be for ever. On the other rare occasions when she had acted normally, it had lasted for at most a day or two but usually for only a few hours.

All I could do was make the most of it. As soon as she emerged from the bedroom, she came over to me, where I was still sitting in the easy chair with my blanket wrapped tightly around me. Her face was still red where Daddy had slapped her, and one cheek was a little bit swollen. Her eyes were puffy the way they always were when she had been crying. There were also blue bruises on her neck and I thought that Daddy must have hit her there as well.

Her voice was very calm when she spoke to me. 'Michael,' she said. 'I don't think we can go on like this. You deserve a lot better – and so do I. I didn't have you so that you would be hurt and miserable and frightened all the time. We've got to get out of here, you and me, even if it's only for a while. We have to do something nice for a change.'

It was the first time Mammy had ever talked about getting away and doing something nice and it sounded wonderful to me.

'I have a friend called John,' she told me. 'He has a nice big car and he has offered to take me and you out for the day if we like. Well, I'm going to speak to him today and tell him that we'd both like that. Would you like that? To go out with someone nice?'

To me it sounded almost too good to be true. 'I'd love that, Mammy,' I told her. 'Just you and me, though. Not Daddy.'

'No, definitely not Daddy,' she said with a kind of shudder. 'It's Daddy we need to get away from.'

20

She led me into the kitchen and took a cloth and bathed my face, which was still coated with dried blood. Then she rubbed some ointment into the cut and put a plaster on my cheek.

I was overjoyed. It was the most attention Mammy had paid me in weeks. Sometimes she went a whole day without speaking a single word to me. And weeks, or so it seemed, without touching me. I found myself actually daring to believe that she might stay normal this time. That my Mammy had actually come back to me.

The next day, she was still acting normally. Daddy hadn't been home. He sometimes stayed away for a day or two after they'd had a big fight and on those occasions Mammy would let me sleep in the big bed with her.

She woke me up bright and early and made sure I washed properly and put clean clothes on. Then she brushed my hair down flat with the big brush she used to do her own hair. My hair was already curly and it took a lot of brushing to make it lie down.

I could feel that she was excited, and I was too. She had put on lipstick and the rest of her make-up and was wearing perfume that smelled sharp and sweet at the same time. That, and the fact she was spending so much time getting me ready, was so rare it had to mean something very special was going to happen. And I was right.

Soon after she had gone down to the shop, a big silver car pulled up outside. I was sitting in the window, from where I liked to look down on the busy street below, and saw it arrive.

A few moments later, Mammy came rushing up the stairs shouting, 'Michael, Michael. It's time to go. Come on, quickly. John is here to take us for a drive in the country.'

I followed her downstairs, where she hung a 'closed' sign behind the glass panel of the door and turned the key behind us.

Mammy's friend was standing by the big silver car, which he told me was called a Jaguar. John was shorter than Daddy, and a bit fatter and had a bald patch, but, unlike Daddy, he gave me a big grin and said he was very pleased to see me and hoped we would become friends.

He opened the back door of the car and suggested I sit there. The back seat seemed very wide and had an armrest in the middle. There was an odd smell, which John explained was the smell of the leather seats. After he had fussed about Mammy and got her settled in the front, John slid in behind the wheel and we were on our way.

The Jaguar was so much more smooth and comfortable than Daddy's second-hand old banger, which used to rattle and shake all the time. It was different from driving with Daddy in other ways too. He hardly ever said a word to us, unless he was in a bad temper and shouting, but John kept up a constant stream of chatter. Mostly he spoke to Mammy, who seemed to be really enjoying herself, laughing out loud at some of his remarks, and sometimes he spoke to me.

John wanted to know all about me, he said. Did I go to school, because I looked so big and grown-up. What games did I like to play? He seemed to be genuinely interested in me and I found myself chattering away in a way that wasn't like me at all. It felt very strange. Normally, when I spoke to people, I said just a few words, and those usually out of necessity. We didn't talk much to one another in our family and I had learned to keep everything hidden away inside. But it was nice talking to John. He had a way of making even the most ordinary things sound funny and he treated me more like a grown-up and not like a little boy.

We eventually stopped in the countryside, where there were no other people, and we sat down beside a stream which gurgled along between grassy banks and big shady trees.

John showed me how to make boats by folding squares of paper and we raced them down the stream, running alongside and whooping and cheering. I managed to fall in twice, but Mammy wasn't cross at all. John said he had fallen into the beck which ran through his village every day when he was young. It was all part of being a boy. Mammy took off my shoes and socks and put them on the grass to dry while we had our picnic. I didn't even mind that the sandwiches were ham and tomato.

I wondered if other boys and girls did this with their parents all the time. It would be so nice to permanently feel this happy, I thought.

All too soon, it was time to go home. By mid-afternoon, we were back in the Ashton Old Road.

John gave me a pat on the head and told me he hoped to see me again soon, so we could play some more games. When I told him I hoped so too, he grinned back at me. Then he kissed Mammy on the cheek and was off.

As soon as we were in the shop, Mammy became very serious. She took me by the shoulders and bent forward so that her face was level with mine. 'This has got to be our secret, Michael,' she told me. 'Nobody must know about our trip with John, especially not Daddy. I know you've enjoyed it, and so have I, and it will be nice if we can do it again. But we won't be able to if Daddy finds out. So you mustn't say a word. Will you promise me?'

'Oh yes,' I said. 'I promise. I won't spoil our secret by telling Daddy. I want to go out with John again. It was fun.'

Over the rest of that summer and autumn, then into winter, John became the only bright spot in my life. From the end of one outing, I would long for the next one.

When it became too cold and wet to visit the countryside, he would take us to other places. One trip was to a museum, another to the zoo. And one of the best was when he took me to a big shop in Manchester to see Father Christmas. He asked me what I wanted for Christmas and I told him I would like a big toy truck. I didn't really expect to get it, though. I was hardly ever given toys for presents, except by Nanny Ramsden, who had given me a football for my birthday.

Daddy always gave me hats as presents, for Christmas and for my birthday. I had a prison warder's hat, a policeman's, a fireman's and various others. They weren't much to play with but I liked them and sometimes lined them up and pretended that people were wearing them and imagined how they would act. Occasionally, Mammy gave me crayons and pencils and drawing books, but neither she nor Daddy ever wanted to look at my drawings.

I had always thought that our outings with John were too good to be true, and I should have known that something that nice wouldn't be allowed to go on. I was a bad boy. Daddy told me that all the time, and I knew that nice things didn't happen to bad boys. Only bad things. But I could never have known just how frightening the consequences of our secret would be.

The beatings from Daddy had gone on throughout the time that John was taking us out, but they were no worse than before. The slaps and the kicks were just as unpredictable and painful, and some of the things he said were still as hurtful, but by now I had almost become accustomed to it all. I'd learned to cope with it. Daddy had always been like that, for as long as I could remember and, at least, since the night he had cut my cheek, he hadn't used the buckle end of his belt on me.

But, on the night we learned he had found out about

our secret trips with John, it was terrifying. I really believed he was going to kill us both.

It was dark when he came home and the fire was burning in the living room, where Mammy and I were watching television. I could tell by the smell of his breath, almost from the moment he came into the room, that he had been drinking, and I was anticipating the usual punishment even before he began to shout.

Mammy, who had gone back to her regular zombie routine in between our outings with John, was only half-awake when Daddy hauled her out of her chair and, with no warning, hit her hard across the face with the back of his hand.

It was so sudden it took us both off guard. Daddy usually had to work himself up into a temper before he started lashing out.

Mammy screamed and fell back in her chair but he just bent forward and gave her another hard slap across the face, which made her scream again.

Then he started to yell just as loudly as her. 'You whore! You dirty, bloody whore! You've been seeing a bloke behind my back. How did you think you could get away with it, eh, you slut? And you took this stupid bastard brat with you. Did you want him to watch you in action? You're a right bloody pair, aren't you! A whore and her bastard son out with her fancy man.'

'He's not a fancy man,' Mammy screamed back. 'He's just a friend who was being nice to us.'

She managed to struggle to her feet and then Daddy

began punching her in the chest. She was screaming more with every blow but he just kept on. He seemed to be out of control.

Then he hit her across the face again and she went crashing down into the fireplace, scattering the fire tongs and brush and knocking over the coal scuttle as she landed hard on her bottom. Her left arm, which was bare almost to her shoulder, struck against the horizontal bars of the iron grate, and suddenly her screams grew even louder.

'You've branded me, you swine!' she shouted.

He laughed at her. 'Serve you right, you bloody whore,' he said, and raised his fist again.

I couldn't stand it any longer. It was far worse than he had ever beaten Mammy before and I was afraid he was going to kill her. I rushed over to him and started kicking his legs and punching at his stomach but it had absolutely no effect on him. He just smashed me across the face with his hand and that took all the fight out of me.

'You bloody little nobody,' he shouted. 'You need to be taught a lesson just like her. One that you won't forget.'

He grabbed me by the arm and neck and hauled me over to the fireplace. Mammy had crawled away and was lying on the carpet, sobbing, and nursing her burned arm in her good hand.

'Let's see if a little of what this slut has had will teach her bastard to behave,' he growled. Then he took my arm and pressed the side of it, between the wrist and elbow, against the hot bars that had burned Mammy.

It was the worst pain I had ever experienced, and I screamed out as loudly as Mammy had done. He held my arm against the grate for a second or two, but the pain seemed to go on for ever, and I could feel the agony everywhere at once – on my arm, in my head, all over. I could smell it too – singed hair and scorched flesh.

When I looked at my arm it had turned bright red and I think a blister was already starting to come up.

I was weeping and probably hysterical, and so was Mammy. Sobbing, she crawled over to me and put her arms around me. She could have been trying to protect me from anything else Daddy might decide to do, or maybe she just needed comforting herself.

The amazing thing is, despite all that screaming, none of our neighbours came to see what was happening, even though they must have heard everything. It was just that kind of place. People minded their own business and nobody ever involved the police. But there was always gossip and everyone in the street knew every detail of one another's lives.

I don't know if Daddy realised he had gone too far or whether he had just run out of steam, but he didn't try to hit us any more. Instead he just glared at us both for a long while and then snarled, 'You two make me sick,' before storming out of the room and down the stairs.

I don't know if he was going back to the pub or to

work. I was simply in such agony that I was just relieved to see him go so that he couldn't hurt me any more.

That is how our secret trips with John came to an end. He never came back to see us in his big Jaguar, and Mammy rarely mentioned his name again. She did tell me that she had first met John on one of her fantasy shopping trips in Manchester. She couldn't afford to buy anything, but she loved to go in the expensive department stores and clothes shops and pretend that she was one of the rich ladies who were shopping there. She always looked at her most beautiful when she was going out on one of these fantasy sprees.

She had met John while having coffee in one of the big stores. He had shared her table and they had started talking. Mammy said he was the first man to treat her like a lady for years and that's why she had agreed to go out with him. He was simply a nice man who had treated her with respect.

But in Openshaw, as in all working-class ghettos, it was impossible to do anything without your neighbours finding out. There were too many eyes.

John had picked us up outside our house at Mammy's insistence. She hoped that by being open about our outings the neighbours wouldn't get the wrong message. But one of them obviously had and, keen to cause trouble, had told Daddy about our secret trips. We never did find out who had betrayed us.

It did achieve one result, though. It made Mammy and me more determined than ever to escape.

Chapter Four

Although we were to carry the scars of Daddy's most brutal attack to date for many years, the actual pain from our burns lasted little more than a week.

The day after my branding, the burn on my arm was a mass of broken, weeping blisters, so Mammy, whose own arm was in much the same condition, took me to the chemist's. There she told me to show my burn to the man behind the counter and asked his advice on what she should put on it.

The chemist wanted to know how it had happened and Mammy told him the story we had concocted that morning before leaving home. She said I had been playing with a ball in the living room and had tripped over and accidentally banged my arm against the hot grate.

'What about the bruise on his face?' the man asked. 'How did he get that?'

'It must have been the same fall,' said Mammy quietly. 'He went head over heels with a big crash.'

The chemist stared hard at me and at Mammy.

'I just tripped over,' I told him.

'And I suppose the bruise on *your* face came from a fall too,' the man said to Mammy.

'Yes,' she replied in almost a whisper. 'A few days ago. I'm as clumsy as the lad.'

I had told similar lies to our neighbours when they had asked about my cuts and bruises, though they probably all knew the truth anyway, but this was the first time I had given a total stranger a made-up story to cover up a beating from Daddy.

I'm sure the chemist didn't believe us but he finally turned away and selected one of the many small boxes that were piled up on the shelves behind him. He gave it to Mammy and told her, 'Put the ointment on twice a day and keep it covered. He looks a healthy enough tyke, so it should heal up fairly quickly. But he needs to be more careful in future. And so do you.'

Mammy didn't say anything. She paid him and almost ran out of the shop, dragging me behind her. Outside, she stopped long enough to blow her nose, and I could see that she was fighting back the tears.

'That man knew,' she said in a trembly voice. 'He knew that I'm married to a wife beater. Everybody knows. But it's not my fault, so why should I have to suffer all the shame? I really don't think I can cope with this much longer.'

But inside I think we both knew that we would have to go on coping. We had nowhere to run to, nowhere to hide. Not at that time anyway.

But that changed for me after I started school, or at least I thought it had.

My fifth birthday was marked by a small party. A handful of local kids came in and we shared a cake that was decorated with five candles, which I managed to blow out in one go. It was the first party I could remember. We never even celebrated Christmas at home. No decorations or tree, not even a cooked meal.

Daddy wasn't there, but Mammy gave me a present, wrapped up in brown paper. I opened it straight away and discovered a small canvas bag with a long strap.

'You'll be going to school after the holidays like a big boy,' Mammy told me, 'and this is your new satchel. You wear it over your shoulder and can carry your school things in it.'

I don't think any child ever looked forward to starting school with more excitement than I did. I imagined it would be just like my days out with John. A safe friendly place, full of nice adventures and out of Daddy's reach.

Our little local Catholic primary school in Openshaw, St Brigid's, was an old Victorian building. I was automatically sent there because my parents were Catholic, even though Daddy was lapsed and Mammy no longer bothered to go to church.

She had taken me on a few occasions to nearby St Anne's Church, a dark and gloomy building with very little lighting inside and dirty walls outside. The first time I was taken there, I was lost. Nobody was allowed to talk unless they were invited to by the priest, who said everything in a funny language I didn't know and which Mammy told me was Latin.

It was something to do with God, but, as there were never religious discussions in our home, I didn't know who God was then. But I liked the smell of the incense and felt very safe there. The feeling that nobody could get at me.

By the time I started school, even these rare visits had stopped, but were replaced by class visits to Mass at the same church on Monday mornings.

I found that many of the kids in our immediate neighbourhood were at my school, some starting with me that year, as well as older ones that I knew from playing in the streets or from the homes I had visited with their younger brothers.

Like most of my clothes, my school uniform was a mixture of new and second hand. Mammy had bought the blazer and grey shorts from a neighbour whose son had grown out of them. My grey V-necked sweater came from a second-hand clothes shop but I had new black shoes and grey socks. On that first day, I felt like a prince in my, to me, new finery. It was as though I really belonged when the final school bell of the afternoon jangled and I joined up in the playground with a crowd of other boys and girls to walk home together.

After that first morning, Mammy never took me to school again, and she was never outside with the other mothers when school turned out in the afternoon.

Some of the other mums found it strange and would ask me where she was, but I never expected her to be there. I used to make up stories about her and Daddy having to do more important things, and after a while people stopped asking me. I was always careful not to tell these tall tales when other kids from my road were about, though I'm sure some of them were telling similar stories to cover up secrets of their own, not to hide the shame of their fathers beating them or their mothers' neglect, but just to conceal the poverty we lived in.

These fantasies took root and grew throughout my school years, as I tried to hide the truth about my nightmare home existence from my teachers and classmates and their parents. As time went by, I became more confident about lying to the teachers about my bruises and other injuries caused by Daddy's beatings. Many of these, though, were in places that were not normally visible.

One of my injuries, more painful than most, happened a few weeks after I started school. It was on a bath night and, as usual, Mammy had half-filled the battered tin bath, which stood on a tattered plastic sheet spread out on the carpet in front of the fire in the living room. She carried the hot water, which was heated by a gas geyser on the kitchen wall, to the bath in a plastic bucket.

I was sitting in the bath and she was soaping my shoulders and back with a flannel when Daddy came in, reeking of beer and with the wide-eyed stare and mean look on his face that usually came before an explosion of temper.

That night was to be no exception. Just the sight of me in the bath seemed to set him off. He must have seen me when he got to the top of the stairs and had already armed himself with a fish slice from the kitchen, which he was slapping against the side of his trousers.

'You've always got time for that little bastard and never any time for me,' he growled at Mammy, who was kneeling on the carpet next to the bath and had to look up at him.

'He's got to have his bath,' she protested meekly.

'Then let the stupid brat bath himself,' he bellowed, and pushed her roughly away by her shoulder.

I felt very exposed sitting naked in the bath, so I stood up and bent over the edge to take the towel from a chair next to where Mammy had been kneeling.

'I'll tell you when you can get out,' Daddy shouted, and raised the fish slice above his head.

I could see him over my shoulder and I knew what was coming, but I had nowhere to escape to. The flat metal end of the implement, which was covered in holes, landed squarely across the bare right cheek of my bottom with a huge thwack, and the force of it shot me over the side of the bath.

I screamed at the top of my lungs and then again as the fish slice connected violently with the other bare cheek of my bottom. The pain was awful. It was as though the whole of my bottom was on fire.

By this time, Mammy was back on her feet. 'Stop it, Joe,' she cried. 'You're going to maim him for life if you carry on. He's only a five-year-old child.'

Daddy's answer was to grab hold of the end of the bath and up-end it over the two of us. Mammy was soaked through and water went everywhere. The bath ended upside down, almost on top of me, and, by the time Mammy had pulled it clear and checked that I wasn't badly hurt, Daddy had done his usual disappearing act.

Mammy flopped down on her bottom on the wet carpet next to me and we both sobbed our hearts out. I had to kneel because I had discovered that sitting was far too painful. When I reached around to rub my sore bottom, I found that it was all lumpy. The fish slice had left its pattern on both buttocks.

That time, like many others, the teachers couldn't see the marks and ask difficult questions, but I spent several very uncomfortable days being unable to sit down without it hurting.

Chapter Five

After this latest beating I was more determined than ever to run away from home, and very soon I believed a real opportunity had come when I heard that the circus was in town.

The big top had been set up on a large bombsite about half a mile along the Ashton Old Road from where we lived. Several gypsy caravans parked there all year round and some of the gypsy children attended my school. Even at my age, I had heard frightening stories about little boys and girls being carried off by the gypsies and never being seen by their families again. When I found out that two of the boys I had palled up with in the playground were gypsies, I remembered the stories and wondered if I might be lucky enough to be stolen.

On one occasion, I had gone back with them to where they lived, to play after school. I had been nervous at first, because of the tales I had heard, but that changed within a few minutes of getting there. The boys were members of two large families, who seemed to have at least four dogs between them and two red-faced, round-cheeked, cheerful mothers who welcomed me with smiles and offers of drinks and biscuits. After my home, it was like being in heaven and I was very sorry when the mother of one of the boys told me to get along home because my own mother would be worrying. There was no point in telling someone nice like her that my mother would not even have noticed I was missing. But it was true.

Mammy had closed the shop and was dozing on the settee. She hardly noticed I had come home at all and didn't even bother to say hello.

I found half a sandwich and a banana in the shop and had my meal in front of the television. Mammy was still asleep on the settee, so I settled myself in an armchair, clutching my thin blanket around me and wishing like mad that I could be back in the gypsy camp with my new friends.

After school the next day, I went back with the same boys and played with them around the big top. To one side of the site was a small cluster of caravans and trailers which housed the circus acts and their families.

My new friends said they didn't know any of the circus children and warned me to keep my distance as some were quite nasty and liked to bully smaller boys.

But I had already decided on a plan and was determined to see it through, so I told them that, if they didn't want to come, I would go on my own and play with the circus children.

I felt brave when I said it, but I didn't feel quite so brave when my new friends all chose to stay behind, yelling after me to be careful and run like mad if I got into a fight.

My idea was not to get into a fight. I wanted the circus people to take me with them when they left town. This was to be my escape route from Daddy and his beatings.

Several boys and girls were standing around by the caravans and most of them looked a lot older than me. Two of the boys nearest to my age were playing with a football and I asked if I could join in.

'Who are you then?' asked one of them. He and his friend stopped kicking the ball and stood in front of me. One or two of the other boys started to wander towards us.

Suddenly I wasn't feeling brave at all.

'I was playing with the gypsy boys and wanted to see the circus,' I told them.

'Does this look like the bloody circus? This is private,' said the boy who had spoken before. 'Outsiders aren't wanted, so bugger off.'

'Maybe he needs a thick ear,' said one of the bigger boys who had joined us. 'Teach him not to come sneaking round here.'

He made a move towards me and I ran. A caravan was

in the way, so I dived under it and rolled to the other side, sprang up and kept running.

I could hear the boys shouting behind me, so I scrambled under the next caravan and crawled behind one of the wheels.

My teeth were chattering now and I was scared the boys would hear me. I could still hear them calling to one another but they hadn't spotted me going under the second caravan, and soon their voices died away. I reckoned they had gone back to the spot where I had first seen them, but I was too frightened to come out of my hiding place.

When I finally plucked up the courage to crawl out from the far side of the caravan there was no one there. It was dark by now and, although I could see the big top, lit up beyond the caravans and trailers and outlined against the black sky, I didn't dare go in that direction in case I ran into the boys who had chased me earlier.

I had never been out after dark by myself before and it was all very frightening. A fine runaway I had turned out to be.

I made my way back to where the gypsies lived. Their mobile homes were all brightly lit inside and I could picture my school friends sitting with their smiling mums having their tea or watching television. I longed to be a part of their world and I was just plucking up the courage to knock on one of the doors when I heard Mammy's voice calling my name.

Moments later, she appeared and I ran over to her and clutched her round the waist. I had never been so happy to see her.

She burst into tears as soon as she saw me, but she was also very angry. She pulled my arms from around her waist and boxed my ears so hard I heard ringing noises in my head. Mammy had never hit me before, except for a slap on the bottom, and the shock was almost as bad as the pain.

I started to cry, and then she pulled me close.

'Oh, Michael,' she said, 'I was so worried about you. One of the gypsy boys came and told Mrs Watson [one of our neighbours] that you had gone off with some older circus boys who were really bad. She came and woke me up and told me, and I came to look for you.'

In that moment, I felt happy. Mammy had been so concerned that she had come out to find me – and that meant she really cared for me. Today, when I think back on it, I suspect she was really more concerned about what the neighbours thought of her mothering skills than about my safety.

But my joy lasted only a few seconds, for Mammy's next words brought all my fear flooding back. 'Daddy'll be home by now and he's going to be mad at you *and* me for being out. I don't know what I'm going to tell him, and, if he sees Mrs Watson before he sees us, then there'll be hell to pay.'

Mammy's hand clung on to mine as she dragged me, so unwillingly, along the Ashton Old Road, the terror building inside me at every step as my imagination conjured up the many awful things Daddy might do to us when we got home.

The house was silent when we went in through the shop and I could hear nothing as we climbed the stairs to the flat, not even the television. My spirits soared. Perhaps Daddy hadn't come home yet.

But when we reached the top of the stairs I could see him sitting on the sofa in the living room, glaring in our direction. When he spoke, I could tell straight away that there had been a subtle shift in his attitude. Whether it was because my mother had dared to go looking for me, which to him would have been tantamount to mutiny, or it was seeing the two of us together like co-conspirators, whatever it was, something that night sent him into a rage the likes of which I'd never seen before.

'What the hell have you been up to, you little nobody?' he snarled at me as he stood up. 'You and your useless mother. You're up to mischief, getting yourself into trouble, and she can't keep you under control. A bloody five-year-old.

'Or perhaps you'd prefer to go with the gypsies too,' he yelled at Mammy. 'You bloody whore. You both need teaching a lesson.'

He had already taken off his belt and must have been sitting there waiting for us, holding it ready, for he was now swinging it, folded double, in his right hand.

Mammy pushed in front of me and took the first blow on her arm. It seemed that this one gesture to protect me was all that was needed to set off his rage. As she screamed and turned away, the next swing of his belt, with its big buckle, caught her right across her buttocks.

I realised then that he was completely out of control. This wasn't his usual calculated bullying. This was a man gone berserk.

As I turned to run and lock myself in the toilet, he grabbed me by the shoulder with his left hand and began beating me on every part of my body with his fist, feet and belt.

The pain got worse and worse and I begged him to stop, but he just carried on swinging and hitting.

When he did take a pause from beating me, he went back to using his belt on Mammy, who was by this time down on her knees with her head on the ground, not even attempting to defend herself, just sobbing.

This complete capitulation by Mammy was more frightening to me than anything my father did to us that night. I realise now that on that night Daddy had finally achieved what must have been his objective – to break her spirit.

When at last he threw his belt on to one of the armchairs, I thought our punishment was over, but I quickly learned differently.

Daddy sometimes carried a black leather-covered baton in a holder fastened to his uniform. It was to use if the prisoners at Strangeways became violent. He drew this out of its holder now and came at me again, jabbing it menacingly in my face and saying quietly, through gritted teeth, 'Maybe a taste of this will teach you to behave in future.'

His face had gone dark red and his eyes were bulging. His colossal anger had become almost tangible.

The first blow of the baton was across my back and its force almost knocked me off my feet. The pain, which was far worse than when he used the belt, seemed to go right through me. He concentrated on beating my back and shoulders – I suppose so that the bruises didn't show – but some of his blows caught me on the arms as well.

It all ended when, perhaps deliberately, or perhaps through poor aim, the baton landed on the side of my head. There was a huge burst of light and lightning like fizzes behind my eyes and then everything went black.

He had managed to knock me senseless.

Just before I passed out, I remember pleading in my head to the powers that be – anything, anyone, any being – to give me one small inkling what it was inside *me* that could provoke such terrible anger and violence from the man who was supposed to be *my* protector – *my* father – and was one day supposed to be my guide into manhood.

How long I was unconscious, I have no idea. Mammy had been so badly beaten with the baton, after he had finished with me, that she was too groggy and in too much pain to know exactly what was happening. But when I came round I was still lying on the floor. I tried to sit up straight away, but my head started spinning so badly I had to lie down again.

Eventually, Mammy managed to crawl to the kitchen and, clinging to the draining board, struggled to her feet. It was difficult to know which of us was the more battered. Finally, she pulled herself together enough to fetch me a cup of water. She had also picked up a dishcloth and soaked it with water under the tap.

Holding me in a sitting position with her arm around my shoulders, she put the cup to my lips. After I had sipped some water, she bathed my face with the wet cloth.

It was then I began to realise that it was me who had come off worse this time, because the roles had been reversed. Usually it was me helping Mammy.

Every bit of me felt tender and I started to cry again and just couldn't stop, even after Mammy helped me up into an easy chair.

It took me a while to notice that Daddy was no longer there, but I was still so frightened by what had happened that I couldn't stop shaking. It was a feeling I was never going to lose while he remained a part of my life. So this new level of fear was to be my daily companion for years to come.

Chapter Six

Daddy's savage attack with his baton did not go unnoticed at school. Suspicious about the cause of my bruises, my class teacher took me to the headmaster's study so that he could examine me.

There was one big bruise on the side of my head, extending almost to the tip of my left eyebrow, and a string of others along my left arm.

Having seen the one on my head, the teacher had rolled up my sleeve before I could stop her, and seen the others. But when she had asked me to take off my shirt I refused, and that must have been what made her so concerned.

'Michael claims he fell downstairs,' she told the headmaster. 'It's the third time this month he's supposed to have fallen downstairs. But I'd say someone has given him a good hiding.'

'Is that right, Michael?' the headmaster asked. 'Did somebody beat you?'

I shook my head violently and was ready with my lie. 'No. Nobody beat me. I just fell downstairs. I'm always doing it. Mammy says I'm clumsy.'

'You're sure your mother or father didn't hit you for being naughty?'

I shook my head again. 'No, sir. It was all my fault. I fell downstairs.'

The headmaster looked at my teacher and nodded. 'All right, you can take him back to the classroom. But I'll have a word with the childcare people just in case. I think they should visit and talk to the parents.'

I could hardly wait to get home that night to give Mammy my news. I didn't stop to play with the other kids but went straight back to the shop, where Mammy was still behind the counter.

'I promise I didn't tell them anything but he said someone might come round,' I blurted.

Mammy looked puzzled. 'What are you talking about, Michael? Who's coming here and what didn't you tell them? Calm down and tell me what happened.'

So I told her all about my visit to the headmaster's study and how they had looked at my bruises and asked if I had been hit by someone.

'But I didn't say it was Daddy,' I told her. 'I told them I had fallen downstairs again. That's what I always say, or that I was hurt in a game or something. I'd never tell them Daddy had done it.'

'Thank God for that,' she gasped. 'And don't say anything to Daddy about what happened at school. It'll only make him more angry than usual. Let's keep this to ourselves for now and wait to see if anyone comes round.

'Perhaps no one will.'

But I think we both knew that was a forlorn hope.

It was more than a week later, but eventually someone did come, a young woman, and she turned up just after I got in from school.

Mammy closed the shop and we all went upstairs. I was told to wait in her bedroom while Mammy and the other woman talked in the living room.

When Mammy came to get me, she was very serious but she wasn't crying, which meant, I thought, that everything was going to be all right.

The woman asked me to take off my shirt and vest and Mammy nodded to show it was OK for me to go ahead. When I had stripped off, the woman told me to turn around so she could see my back.

By this time, most of my bruises were either a bit yellow or had nearly disappeared, though I think there were still quite a lot of them; enough anyway to make the social worker ask a lot of questions.

'I fell downstairs,' I kept telling her, but I don't think she believed me any more than the teachers had.

'These look like they came from much harder knocks

than you would get just falling downstairs,' she told us. 'What really happened?'

'I fell downstairs,' I repeated.

'He's always falling downstairs,' said Mammy. 'He's in such a hurry to get out and play with his friends he doesn't take care. I keep telling him to slow down but at five they don't take much notice, do they?'

The social worker obviously didn't believe us, but there was clearly not a lot that she could do about it.

If we just keep on telling lies, eventually she will go, I thought.

In the end, that's what happened. The woman stood up and told Mammy, 'I'm not entirely happy with the explanations you've both given me. I don't think I'm hearing the whole story. I may decide to have Michael examined by a doctor, and I'm also going to want to see you both again in the future. I'll probably make it an evening so that I can talk to your husband as well, Mrs Seed.'

I don't think Mammy or I was happy with that. Except that perhaps Daddy would become angry and hit the social worker and they would take him away. That would be good.

After Mammy had seen the woman out, she came back upstairs and said, 'Oh, Michael, I feel so ashamed. What are we going to do? They only send social workers to check up on the worst possible kind of families. If my mother or father ever found out, they'd be horrified.'

Secretly, I was quite happy with the situation.

Especially after Mammy told Daddy about the visit. Whatever she said had a big effect on him. He didn't stop shouting at us, but for at least a couple of weeks I didn't receive his regular thrashings. It seemed he was just as terrified about people finding out the truth of the situation as she was.

The effect on Mammy was much more worrying. She became even more switched off, if that was possible. Sometimes she would be crying when I left for school in the morning and still crying when I came home. I don't know if she opened the shop in the afternoons at all, because she always seemed to be upstairs, crying or sitting in a chair just staring into space.

But one day she did something which was very different indeed and it left me terrified.

I had returned home from school at the normal time and found the shop already closed. That in itself was no longer unusual as Mammy had been acting more strangely since the social worker's visit and seemed to have totally lost interest in the shop.

When I went upstairs, she was sprawled out in the armchair in a funny way. Her legs seemed to be bent at an odd angle and her arm was flopped over the side of the chair, just dangling down. She seemed to be asleep but I could tell that something wasn't quite right. For some reason, it frightened me and I did something I had never done before. I shook her and tried to wake her up. But she didn't move.

I shook her really hard by the shoulders and even

pulled at her hair, but she stayed fast asleep. Her mouth was slightly open and she was breathing with a rasping sound.

'Mammy, wake up!' I shouted in her ear, but she didn't even twitch. Nothing I did had the slightest effect on her. I began to feel really scared. I had seen her in a zombie-like state before but never flopped out like this, unable to wake up. She just didn't look right.

I don't know how long I had been trying to wake her, but it was a long time after I had come home when I heard Daddy on the stairs.

For once, I was overjoyed to see him, though he was about as pleased to see me as ever. He had always allowed his contempt for me to show, but, since the last beating and the social worker's visit, it seemed as though he was now giving free rein to his bullying and hatred, but without the physical violence.

After all, who was going to stop him? Certainly not poor Mammy, who was lying, broken and battered on the settee.

'What are you snivelling about, you little bastard?' he spat.

Until then, I hadn't realised that I was crying.

'It's Mammy,' I said. 'She won't wake up. I've been shaking and calling her for ages but she stays asleep.'

Daddy stopped glaring at me and pushed me to one side, though not roughly for once. He knelt down next to where Mammy was sitting and gently shook her arm. Even I could detect the anxiety in his voice as he whispered, 'Lillian, come on, Lillian, wake up, for Christ's sake, woman. It's Joe here. Your Joe.'

Never before had I heard him use such a tender tone to her. He laid the side of his face gently on her breast.

'Wake up, Lillian, love. Wake up, will you.'

But Mammy just lay there dead to the world, as she had been since I'd got home from school.

Daddy moved round in front of her and took her by the shoulders and pulled her forward.

I grabbed his arm and cried, 'Please don't hurt her any more. She's only asleep.'

'I'm not hurting her,' he said. 'I have to lift her up so I can get her downstairs and into the car. She needs to go to hospital.'

Then he reached down and picked up one of Mammy's pill bottles, which had been lying on the floor. He shook it but there was no rattling sound. It must have been empty.

'I'd better take this with me to show them,' he muttered, and put the bottle in his pocket. Then he lifted Mammy up, knelt in front of her, and let her fold forward, face downwards over his shoulder, with her head lolling against his back.

He told me not to go out but to stay where I was until he got back. 'I don't know how long I'll be,' he said as he carried her downstairs. 'But I'll be back.'

I heard the back door slam and ran to the front window. A couple of minutes later I saw his car turn out of the side street into the Ashton Old Road.

I sat on the sofa and tried to stay awake, hoping they would come home together as though nothing had happened. But I must have dropped off to sleep, because when Daddy woke me it was morning.

'Where's Mammy?' I asked him, rubbing my eyes.

'They're keeping her in hospital for a day or two. She's not very well, but she's going to be all right. You'll just have to get yourself to school and I'll be back this evening after I've visited your mother. The key will be with her next door. Get yourself something to eat and don't bring anyone home with you. Understand?'

'Yes,' I told him, and that was it. I would have to fend for myself. But what was new in that?

It wasn't until two days later, at school, that I learned my Mammy had tried to kill herself. One of the neighbour's boys had heard his mother telling the details to another neighbour. Mammy had taken a huge overdose of her depression pills because she wanted to die, he told me. He obviously thought it was a fabulous piece of gossip to spread around the school.

To me, it was devastating. Mammy dead. I just couldn't imagine it. She would never leave me alone with Daddy. It couldn't be true.

'You're lying,' I screamed. 'My mammy wouldn't want to die and leave me.'

'It's true,' he cried, a satisfied smirk on his face. 'I know it's true 'cos it was your dad who told my mam about it in the first place. I heard her say so.'

It was like the bottom had fallen out of my world.

Chapter Seven

The thought of Mammy being dead was to haunt me for the next three years – until finally reality over took imagination.

Nothing else and nobody else seemed to matter any more. Certainly not my school lessons. In that first year at primary school, a learning pattern began that I was to follow for most of my school life.

I didn't see the point of studying if Mammy could die and leave me so easily and abandon me, on my own, to cope with Daddy's brutality. It all seemed a complete waste of time. So I shut down.

When other children struggled to master their ABC, I simply sat there looking at the pictures, and when it came to writing things down I covered the paper with scribble.

What my teachers thought about me didn't concern me. Not that they seemed to be worried by my lack of effort. As long as I was quiet and didn't disrupt the class, as some children did, they were apparently happy to let me scribble away.

The first year was not important anyway, I heard some of them say. Plenty of time later on for me to learn to read and write. Not one person, at school or at home, appeared in the slightest bit concerned that I was well on my way to becoming the class dunce. Least of all me. I had far more important things to worry about.

The second time I returned home from school and found the shop closed and Mammy upstairs asleep in an armchair, it was much more frightening. From the moment I discovered that the shop door was locked and saw the closed sign in the window, things that had never worried me in the past, I immediately started to picture the scene upstairs. Would I find her like she was before, and would she be alive or dead this time?

By the time I had run round to the back door and was inside, by the bottom of the stairs, I was almost too frightened to go up, in case my worst suspicions turned out to be correct.

Eventually, I managed to overcome my fears and crept up the stairs, until my eyes were level with the landing and I could look along into the living room.

When I first saw her sitting in the armchair everything looked perfectly normal, the way I had found her asleep dozens of times before at this stage of the day.

But, as I walked along the landing and got closer to her, I could see that there was something very odd, unnatural, about the way she was sitting. Her legs were awkwardly splayed outwards and one of her arms, as before, was over the edge of the chair and just dangling.

My heart began hammering away inside my chest and my breath seemed to catch as I sucked in air. Suddenly, I was terrified that she might be already dead.

It was a big effort to make my legs carry me on towards her and, even when I was very close, and could see and hear her breathing, it wasn't much better. My teeth were rattling with fear. I had already dropped my school bag, and now I grabbed her by the shoulder with both hands and began to shake her as hard as I could.

I shouted, 'Wake up, Mammy. Wake up. Please wake up.'

But she just sat there, her head lolling backwards and forwards and sideways as I shook her, and her eyes remained tightly closed.

I didn't know what else to do. I couldn't take her to hospital myself and I knew that, if I went to fetch a neighbour to help, Daddy would be angry. He wouldn't like it at all. Even though it was he who had told a neighbour about the last time Mammy had taken too many pills, I also remembered that he had shouted at her and slapped her for talking to them about our private family affairs.

On the other hand, I couldn't just do nothing and let Mammy die, and I realised that she did need to go to hospital – and quickly. It was a terrible dilemma to be in, and at five I had never been faced with that kind of big decision before.

Just to be doing something, I went to the kitchen and soaked a tea towel under the cold tap and took it back to the living room and bathed her face. But she didn't budge. And now her breathing sounded worse. It was slower, but louder, a kind of hoarse sound as though she was fighting for breath.

I kept on shaking her and shouting in her ear for her to wake up, and finally I was on the point of going to seek help from a neighbour when I heard Daddy come in downstairs.

I didn't wait for him to come up, but ran over to the top of the stairs and shouted down to him. 'She's done it again. Mammy won't wake up. She's dying. Please come and stop her dying, Daddy. Will you, please?'

He ran up the stairs and dashed straight over to where Mammy was sitting — as she had been for what seemed to me like an age. This time he didn't waste any time but bent down and hauled her up on to his shoulder and carried her, not to the stairs as I had expected, but to the kitchen.

He told me to drag an ordinary chair close to the sink and dumped Mammy down on it, on her bottom, and turned her slightly sideways so that her head was towards the sink.

After making sure she was balanced properly and wasn't going to topple over on to the floor, he went to one of the low cupboards and pulled out a large jug.

He filled this with cold water and then poured in half a packet of table salt, which he stirred in with a wooden spoon.

'They used a stomach pump at the hospital, but this should have the same effect if we can get it down her,' he said.

He tilted back her head and held her nose until her mouth opened and poured in some of the mixture. Mammy looked so helpless and pathetic, more like a broken toy than a person. Until then, she hadn't reacted at all to anything we had done.

Some of the liquid ran down her chin and on to her dress, but some of it must have gone down her throat because she started to choke. Daddy put her head over the sink and began slapping her on the back. She made coughing noises but nothing much else happened. So he repeated the whole thing, pouring more of the salt solution down her throat until she sort of convulsed and a whole torrent of stuff burst out of her mouth and all over the sink and on to the window sill behind.

It made me feel sick just to watch it, but, as soon as she stopped heaving, Daddy lifted her head back and gave her another huge dose of salt water.

She was violently sick again, and so it went on, with Daddy repeating the process until Mammy was only bringing up water. Only then did he give her a drink of clear water. And this she managed to keep down.

'That should have got all the shit out of her stomach,' said Daddy. 'Now, if we can get her moving for a while, we'll be able to let her sleep it off. Apart from that, there's not much more that we, or anyone else, can do for her now. But, if we got it out of her in time, she should be all right.'

'Does that mean she's not going to die?' I asked him through my sobs, because I had been crying ever since he came home.

'I don't think she will,' said Daddy. 'But God knows what she's done to her brain, taking all those pills. Until she wakes up, we're not going to know for certain.'

It didn't sound all that hopeful to me but I had to trust Daddy to know what he was doing. And, even with everything else going on, I was thinking that this was about the longest talk I had ever had with Daddy without him hitting me.

'Let's try and get her walking,' he said.

He placed her right arm around his neck and put his left arm around her waist and hauled her to her feet, supporting her weight against his hip. The first time he tried to set her on her feet, her legs buckled under her, but he hung on and kept her upright and then half-carried her, half-dragged her around the living room until she eventually began to move her legs herself and tried to support her own weight.

It must have been hard for Daddy, strong as he was, but he kept on circling the room with her until she was walking almost normally. Then he guided her into the bedroom and lowered her gently on to the bed. He lifted up her feet and straightened her and she immediately rolled over on to her side, tucked her knees up and her elbows close to her chest and fell asleep.

'Now it's up to nature to take its course,' Daddy told me. 'Go and see what you can find to eat downstairs and then you'd better get to bed.'

I could scarcely believe it: Daddy thinking about me eating and getting me to go to bed. I ran downstairs and found part of a loaf of bread, a piece of cheese and some tomatoes and took them upstairs, where Daddy made us sandwiches.

We sat and ate them in front of the television watching a quiz show, though I was far too excited to pay much attention. Sitting and eating with Daddy was a completely new experience. I almost forgot that Mammy might still be dying in the bedroom. It had been a day of big surprises all round.

Next morning, Mammy was up before I went to school, looking very white and sickly and not saying very much.

'I'm sorry, Michael,' she told me. 'Sorry you had to go through all that again.'

But she didn't appear to be very happy to be alive. Certainly not happy enough to stop her trying to kill herself again. And again.

For over the next few months the upstairs drama was to become an almost regular feature of our family life. Usually, Daddy was able to cope, and when I found her unconscious I waited for him to come home.

On one other occasion, though, he wasn't able to

make her vomit up the pills and had to take her to hospital to have her stomach pumped out. At other times, he managed to cope alone by giving her the salt-water treatment.

Before my seventh birthday, Mammy was to try an amazing total of nine times to kill herself by overdosing with pills.

I don't know why the doctors kept giving them to her, or perhaps Daddy wasn't telling them or she was buying other pills from the chemist, but she didn't succeed in killing herself. What she did do was become more and more unhappy and depressed.

Chapter Eight

Mammy's repeated attempts at suicide provided irresistible ammunition for the kids at St Brigid's, who, with typical childish malevolence, nicknamed her 'Suicide Lil'. Sometimes a group of these tormentors would surround me in the playground chanting things like, 'Old Suicide Lil, she keeps taking the pill.'

At that age, I'm not sure if they understood what it was they were saying, but that didn't make my distress any easier to endure. It was so easy for teachers and other adults to say, 'Words can't hurt you', but I can only assume that, as five-year-olds, they had never experienced the misery of their mother's repeated attempts to kill herself and then been forced to suffer their classmates' persecution over it.

It didn't take much of this torture for me to start hating the other kids at school, and what few friendships I had formed by that age quickly fizzled out under the daily verbal onslaught in the playground and classroom. I wasn't a coward by any means, but I knew I couldn't fight them all. So I took the only way out open to me. I became a loner.

I stopped talking to my classmates or trying to join in their games. I became an outcast by choice, although, in truth, few of them wanted my company anyway. It was a role I was to perfect during the remainder of my wretched childhood.

I think I could have coped better had some of the boys chosen to physically attack me. I didn't look for pain, but I had learned to handle far worse beatings than any of my classmates could have handed out. It was the verbal bullying that was so wounding. Yet I was determined I would never give my tormentors the satisfaction of seeing me cry. I did most of my crying when I was alone.

One evening, after a particularly hurtful day at school, I was so upset I stupidly mentioned it to Daddy. I should have had more sense and known from past experience that he would be far from sympathetic.

He immediately turned on me, his eyes starting from his head. 'You're such a spineless wimp,' he snarled. 'You should stand up to them. Not come snivelling home like a bloody girl. You're useless. Not worth a bloody damn. No real son of mine would act like that. But then it's probably your fault your mother is trying to kill herself in the first place. It certainly isn't mine.'

I gasped out loud. Daddy had said a lot of awful things to me in the past, but this was the nastiest thing ever.

'If it wasn't for you coming into our lives. things would never have got this bad,' he said harshly.

I began to cry. I couldn't help it. Could Daddy be right? Was I really the reason Mammy was trying to kill herself? I turned to where she was sitting, on the sofa as usual, hoping she would deny what Daddy had said. But it was one of her switched-off times. Her eyes were open and I knew she was awake but she appeared to be taking no notice of anything going on around her.

'What a bloody useless pair,' Daddy snarled. 'A clapped-out tart and a stupid little bastard.'

Then Mammy spoke. That in itself was amazing, because in that state she rarely said a word. But more amazing to me was what she said.

'Don't upset your father any more, Michael. You'll only make him angry and then you know what will happen.'

Daddy laughed out loud, a nasty mocking sound, and he slapped me hard across the face. 'See what I mean,' he crowed. 'Your mother knows it's your fault as well.' And he hit me again across the other side of my face, knocking me off my chair.

I was in total shock. Not from the slaps, which I was used to, but from what Mammy had said. Surely she didn't really blame me for all our troubles. It wasn't me who was making her try to kill herself. I desperately needed her to tell me I was wrong, but she just sat there, silent, back in her zombie state.

'It's not my fault,' I screamed at Daddy. 'It's not.'

His answer was to kick me in the side, the casual way he might have kicked aside a piece of old rubbish. It knocked the wind out of me and I felt quite dizzy for a few moments, though instinct and experience made me curl into a ball in case there was more to come.

'You're useless,' he shouted. 'A complete waste of space,' and he kicked me again, this time on my thigh.

I screamed and my sobs became even louder. I could feel the tears washing down the side of my face and on to the floor. The pain in my side was getting worse all the time and I thought that, if Daddy kicked me there again, I would probably die.

But he had apparently tired of the sport of treating me like a football and, after a last half-hearted kick to my bottom, he stomped downstairs and took off.

I lay on the floor for ages and, when I eventually tried to sit up, there was a deep stab of pain from my side, which made me gasp out loud. I lifted my shirt and saw that the area around where he had kicked me was already turning bluey-purple and I knew it would turn into a massive bruise. As so often, it was not in a place where anyone would see it.

Eventually, I managed to get back on my chair at the little table and I rested my head on my arms. On the sofa, Mammy kept staring at nothing.

I had never felt so utterly lonely in my life. I couldn't think of anyone in the whole world who was likely to offer me so much as a kind word – except perhaps my Nanny Ramsden, and we hadn't been to see her for more than a year.

If anyone had to die, I thought, it ought to be Daddy, and I sat there wishing with all my being that he would die that night. Right then. Wherever he was. That he would never come home again.

But at that moment I heard his steps on the stairs and was suddenly terrified. What if he had somehow felt what I was wishing and had come back to punish me. It was very unusual for him to come back after he had handed out a beating and left the house.

I would have dived to hide behind the sofa but my side was still hurting too badly for me to move that quickly. So I kept my head on my arms and closed my eyes and pretended to be asleep.

Chapter Nine

The summer before my sixth birthday seemed more than usually sunny and I spent most of my time playing in the back yard or in the lanes with other boys from the neighbourhood.

Despite our shared concern over Mammy's suicide attempts, my relationship with Daddy had not been improved, and whenever she tried again he either ignored me or cursed me as usual.

The beatings kept on but now when he was mad he tended to concentrate his anger on me rather than on Mammy. Not that he gave up hitting her entirely. But her black eyes and split lips became less frequent as his attacks on me intensified. I was still not certain why I was being so severely punished. But at the same time I had been told so often that I was a bad and stupid child I supposed it had to be true and therefore I deserved to be beaten.

Yet, before I celebrated my sixth birthday, my relationship with Daddy was to become even more weird and cruel. It was something that troubled me greatly at the time and is still able to stir very strong emotions even now.

No doubt he was struggling to cope with the breakdown of his marriage and Mammy's awful depression and suicide attempts, but even so I found it hard, in my heart, until many years later, to forgive him for taking repeated advantage of my age and innocence. There is no possible excuse for the way he forced me to take part in his perverted actions. What he did was morally corrupt and utterly indefensible.

The beatings and my constant fear of being attacked were difficult enough to endure, but the new element he introduced into our relationship created a different and much more pervasive fear in me. And, because the threat was never clearly defined, it was all the harder to bear.

It began shortly after the second time Mammy tried to end her life. Now, even when awake, she was far less responsive than before and spent most of the time in a kind of permanent dream which cut her off from everyday life.

Unless Daddy insisted and dragged her there, which he now did less and less often, she no longer made any attempt to sleep in the bed she had previously shared with him.

Instead, she took over my customary place on the sofa, wrapping herself in Daddy's old RAF great coat, which normally acted as a blanket on their bed, and I was demoted to sleeping in one of the armchairs.

But, one night, when Mammy was in one of her now habitual drug-induced stupors, Daddy told me I was not to sleep in the chair but to go into the big bedroom and wait for him.

I have never, for one moment in my life, ever forgotten the most minute and horrific detail of every single second of what was about to happen, and yet, in the 45 years since it first happened, I have never mentioned it to another soul. I only do so now, in all its gross and awful detail, not to shock, but in the hope that others, facing similar torment, can identify with me and start to believe that there is some hope in the future.

My father's order to go to his bed seemed a weird one but I did as I was told, knowing from experience that showing the slightest reluctance to comply with anything Daddy wanted was likely to unleash another brutal attack.

I was wearing my pants and vest as normal for sleeping, but when he came into the bedroom he told me to strip off completely before getting into bed. The sheets were quite chilly, so I snuggled down and clutched the meagre bedclothes around me and settled down for sleep.

But Daddy had other plans. He undressed until he was also completely naked before switching off the light and climbing into bed.

For some reason, I felt very nervous and wriggled nearer the edge of the bed until I was almost hanging over the floor.

Daddy just lay there silently on his back, next to me, for several minutes. When he did speak to me, it was in a voice I barely recognised. It was really strange. There was none of the usual harshness. He spoke quietly and in a slightly lighter tone. Not like Daddy at all. He told me I was there to do some milking. He had to produce milk and I was going to help him. I had absolutely no idea what he was talking about and didn't utter a word. I just couldn't work out how we were supposed to do milking in bed.

Then his hand touched my arm and he slid it down until it covered my hand, which he started to pull towards him. I don't know why but suddenly I felt even more nervous. I think I knew instinctively that we were embarking on something that was very wrong.

'I'll show you what to do,' Daddy told me. 'It's very easy. Very simple.'

He carried my hand across until I felt the bare skin on his thigh and then he pressed my hand against a hard object. I knew straight away that it must be his willy. But it was long and very stiff and sticking straight up. I tried to take my hand away but he grabbed my wrist and forced it back.

'Do what I tell you – or you'll regret it,' he snarled in the voice he normally used with me.

Now I knew for certain that this wasn't supposed to be happening. But I was far too frightened not to do as he wanted.

He told me to put my hand around his willy and then he closed his hand over the top of mine. I was amazed at how large his willy was. I had never noticed it being this big when he was dressed. It was so big my fingers only just closed around it.

Then, with his hand still clamped over mine, he began to rub it up and down.

'Do you think you can do that by yourself, Michael?' he asked, again in that funny non-Daddy voice he had used earlier.

'Yes,' I told him.

There was nothing else I could have said. I was almost breathless with fear. I was in totally unexplored territory. The whole thing was completely bizarre and I was scared silly.

I began to pump my hand up and down, and after he had moved it further up, towards the end of his willy, he took away his hand completely.

'You mustn't stop until the milk comes,' he told me. 'Whatever happens, you mustn't stop until I tell you.'

After a while, my hand started to get tired, but I didn't dare stop. Daddy had ordered me not to, and I had so many bruises on my body to remind me what would happen if I didn't obey him and made him angry.

Suddenly he threw the sheet and thin blanket back and began to breathe heavily. 'Keep going,' he told me in a hoarse voice. 'The milk is about to come.'

Then he gave a great groan and a long sigh and I felt warm liquid splash on to my hand and arm.

Daddy's hand clamped over mine again and kept it moving for a few moments longer, then he pulled my hand free and pushed me hard away from him, back towards the edge of the bed.

I lay there very still and kept as far away from him as I could, listening as his breathing became less noisy.

He didn't say anything else and I assumed that the milking must have been successful. It had been the strangest experience of my life, but I figured that probably all daddies needed milking from time to time, and that it was quite normal for them to get their sons to help them. To me, it was a very odd explanation, but it was the only one I could come up with.

In the morning, Daddy's voice was back to normal and he was already dressed when he woke me. He told me to sit on the edge of the bed and listen to him very carefully. He remained standing in front of me and I felt very small and vulnerable as I looked up at him.

'This is something we don't talk about to anyone else,' he told me sternly. 'It's our secret and must not be shared even with Mammy. If you ever mention this to another soul, then awful things will happen to you. Worse things than you could ever imagine.'

This was the most dreadful kind of threat, precisely

because it wasn't spelled out. I had a very vivid imagination as a five-year-old and, if Daddy was threatening something worse than I could imagine, I knew it had to be very bad indeed.

Of course, at that time, I had no idea that what had happened was a sexual act, or that by involving me in his 'milking' he was guilty of abuse. I had nothing to compare it with. I thought this was something that grown-ups did. None of the boys I knew had mentioned doing anything like this with their fathers, but I also assumed that, if their fathers had issued the same threats to them as mine had to me, this was probably the reason it wasn't talked about.

After that first night, it became quite normal for me to be sent to sleep in the big bed, and if Mammy ever thought this was odd she kept it to herself. Milking Daddy became a fairly regular chore. Sometimes it would happen every night of the week. He would come to bed and wake me up and make me do things and afterwards I would be allowed to sleep again.

I didn't realise until many years later, when it was far too late, that Daddy had made me his sex slave. How could I have known? I knew instinctively that what Daddy was making me do was wrong, but I didn't know why he wanted me to do it and, apart from those gasping moments just before he produced the milk, he appeared to get very little pleasure from it.

He never thanked me for my efforts at the time and they were never mentioned outside of the bedroom.

Nor did it bring us any closer together or lessen his animosity towards me. He still appeared to hate me with a passion and continued to beat me for no apparent reason; apparent to me, that is. For Daddy to believe that I was a bad boy seemed to me reason enough for him to go on hurting me.

My teachers clearly shared Daddy's opinion as, after I turned six, I was old enough to be caned – something that didn't happen in the first year. Caning appeared to be an integral part of the teaching programme at St Brigid's. We were regularly lined up and every girl and boy slashed across the palm of the hand with a long, narrow bamboo wand. Some teachers preferred to cane the bottom and some chose to slap the back of our heads. Either way, it was all part of the daily routine for a six-year-old and something none of us ever thought to complain about.

We were caned because we were naughty. That was the way things were. We had no choice in the matter.

Chapter Ten

L ife with Daddy was never what you could call predictable. His rages now came with little warning, and the level of damage he inflicted on both Mammy and myself varied in keeping with his mood swings. But, by the time I was six-and-a-half, I thought I knew all the telltale signs and could more or less recognise whether it was the mild or the malevolent Daddy who had come home to us.

Then he added a new factor to the battleground which was our home life and I was lost again.

He arrived home one evening with a carrier bag in hand and announced that he had bought us tea, even though it was well after the time we normally had our meal.

Mammy and I had already eaten our usual sandwiches, and I'd had a banana as well, and she told Daddy she wasn't hungry at all.

'You and Michael go ahead and eat,' she said, and went back to dozing on the sofa.

Daddy fetched two plates and knives and forks from the kitchen and put them on the little table in the living room.

'Come and sit down,' he told me, and took a paper-wrapped packet out of the carrier bag.

The moment it was opened my heart sank. That Daddy should bring home food for our meal was unique in itself. With my luck, I might have known that he would have chosen something I couldn't eat.

Fish and chips. Other children loved them, and I too enjoyed the chips and the batter wrapped around the fish. But I found the fish itself revolting. I had never liked its slimy texture, its taste or its smell.

Daddy, after adding salt and vinegar and tomato ketchup, tucked into his meal with obvious pleasure.

I took my time over the chips and picked at the batter, hoping that Daddy would finish quickly and go out. But, after he had eaten everything on his plate, he sat opposite me and stared at my remaining food. Eventually, there was no batter left and the white flesh sat untouched in the middle of my plate.

'I want you to eat that up,' he told me, pointing at the fish with his knife.

'But I don't like fish, Daddy,' I said.

He stood up, came around the table and stood behind me and hissed, 'Eat it now.'

I started to cry. Partly because I was scared at what Daddy might do next and partly in the slight hope that it would put him off. Tears had never saved me before but it still seemed worth a try.

He rapped me hard on top of the head with his knife and put his mouth right next to my ear and shouted, 'Eat the bloody fish, you little bastard.'

'I can't,' I shouted back.

'We'll see about that,' he said, and slapped me hard on both sides of my head.

I screwed my head round to see if Mammy would come to my aid but Daddy was in the way. Suddenly, he grasped the hair at the back of my head and forced my mouth and nose into the fish. I kept my mouth shut but some of the fish was forced into my nostrils and, when I tried to breathe, I snorted some of it back into my throat. Mixed in with this was the feel and smell of blood. My nose had started to bleed when he had rammed it down on the plate.

My stomach reacted immediately and I felt the whoosh of sick in my mouth. But Daddy was pressing my head down so hard it couldn't come out. And I couldn't suck any air in either.

I started to hammer my fists up and down on the table top and bang my feet on the floor in terror, until at last he let go of my hair.

As I raised my face from the plate and opened my

mouth to breathe, all the sick shot out on to the plate and table before I could inhale. When I eventually sucked in some air, I deliberately blew it out down my nose to try to get rid of the fish that had lodged there.

Bits of fish and blood added to the filthy mess already in front of me and this brought a roar of anger from Daddy. He slapped my head back and forth with his open palm and then dragged me by my collar towards the fire.

I screamed, 'Mammy, don't let him burn me. Please don't let him burn me,' but she just sat there. Perhaps she had switched off when Daddy began shouting and didn't understand what was happening, but I felt utterly abandoned.

And when I looked up at Daddy he was actually half smiling.

'Let's see if this will teach you to do as you're told,' he said.

I could feel the heat coming off the fire from several feet away and knew from the last time he had branded me just how awful the pain was going to be. At least I thought I did. But this time it was far worse than I'd imagined.

He pulled my shirt sleeve up my arm, tearing the button off the cuff with the force. Then, with both hands, he grasped my arm at the elbow and the wrist and pressed the middle bit against the top bar of the grate.

It sizzled and the hairs on my arm were singed away and there was a smell of me burning. I screamed and screamed and wet my trousers. The pain was worse than anything that had ever happened to me before.

After a couple of seconds, Daddy pulled my arm away from the fire and pushed me towards the kitchen.

'Stop that screaming, you dirty little brat,' he shouted. 'And get yourself cleaned up. You're disgusting. When you've cleaned yourself up, then clean up the table and the floor where you've made a mess. You're not fit to call a boy. You're like a bloody animal, and that's the way I'm going to treat you in future, like a bloody animal.'

After I had washed my face and changed my trousers for a dry pair, I got out a bucket and cloth and cleaned up the mess in the living room. My only relief came when I scraped the fish into the dustbin. At least I hadn't given in. But at what a cost.

I quietly sobbed myself to sleep in the corner and later, after Daddy had led Mammy off to their bedroom, I went into the kitchen and found the remains of the burn ointment Mammy had got from the chemist after the first time Daddy had burned us.

I smeared it on my blistered arm and swore to myself that one day I would get my revenge – or run away.

Meanwhile I dreaded our next encounter, because, knowing Daddy, he would not let it end like this. Forcing me to eat food I hated was a new way of punishing me, and he wouldn't stop after only one victory. Sure enough, attempts to force-feed me became a regular feature of our violent confrontations.

Chapter Eleven

For me life was a battle for survival. I had no idea what Daddy was fighting for. Or why he had so much anger against Mammy and me. I told myself I must be the baddest boy in the world to warrant so much punishment.

In her rare lucid moments Mammy would try to reassure me. 'You're not really a bad boy, Michael,' she would say. 'Daddy doesn't mean all the things he says and does. It's just his rages. He gets so angry he doesn't even realise he's hurting you. Deep down he loves you really.'

But it was very hard to remember that Daddy loved me when he was in the middle of knocking me senseless or branding me on the grate.

Mammy also blamed Daddy's drinking. She had been brought up strictly temperance, she told me. Which meant, she was proud to say, that alcohol had never passed her lips.

'The devil is cunning and uses alcohol to gain easy entry into a drinking man's mind,' she said.

I think the devils who had such easy access to Daddy's mind must have had a special dislike for Mammy and me, because I never heard of him hitting anyone else when he was drunk.

After the fish incident, Daddy made a point, at least once a week, of bringing home for my tea something that he knew I didn't like. Brawn was his next choice. This cold meat dish, not eaten much outside the north of England, is made from all the unwanted and unmentionable bits of animals that no one would ever dream of eating. Guts, fat, gristle, bone and skin are cooked up and disgusting brown jelly holds it all together in a lump.

Mammy had once tried it out on me and my stomach had rebelled after just a tiny taste. Knowing this, Daddy bought some sliced brawn for my tea. He put two whole slices of the revolting concoction on a plate, which he ordered me to eat. There was lots of goodness in it, he told me with a nasty sneer.

'So why aren't you eating it as well?' I asked him, and instantly regretted it. Daddy was the very last person who needed any provocation.

'Don't be so bloody cheeky,' he snarled. 'Get it down

you now or I'll have to force it down and you won't like that, I can tell you.'

This time I didn't have Mammy for support or even as a silent witness. She had scuttled away downstairs to the shop moments after Daddy had appeared on the landing.

I didn't blame her, because given the slightest chance I would have disappeared out of his way myself, and I knew quite well that she couldn't have helped me anyway. It was just that, if she was sitting near by, even when she was drugged up and barely conscious, I didn't feel quite so utterly alone and vulnerable.

I cut a small piece from one of the mosaic-like slices and speared it on the end of my fork. In the jelly were bits of skin with hair still on and it made me feel sick just to look at it. My stomach heaved at the thought of swallowing it, and I knew there was absolutely no way I was going to be able to put that horrid muck into my mouth.

So I simply sat there staring at it on the end of my raised fork, and I began to cry. Big tears tumbled down my cheeks and splashed on to the table. From experience, I knew that something very bad was going to happen and there was nothing I could do to stop it. I was very scared.

Daddy carried on glaring at me across the little table and then slowly, without looking, he reached down below table height as though he was feeling for something. Moments later, my dread leaped up several notches, when his hand reappeared holding his shiny black baton. He raised it all the way to shoulder height and suddenly slammed it down on to the table with a bang. My plate jumped several inches in the air and I leaped up from my chair in sheer fright, then slowly sat again as Daddy placed his baton on my shoulder and pressed me down.

'Now, are you going to eat your tea or do I have to find a way to feed you?' Daddy asked in a fairly normal voice.

'I can't,' I cried. 'I just can't eat it. I'll be sick. Please don't make me eat it.'

I didn't expect him to take much notice of my pleas because he never did. But I certainly hadn't anticipated what happened next.

My left hand was still holding the fork and my right hand was palm down on the table beside my plate.

Daddy simply raised the baton and, in one swift, deliberate movement, brought it crashing down on the back of my hand.

The shock forced all the breath out of me with a whoosh. Then came the pain, which seemed to race up my arm like something alive. I tucked my injured hand under my left armpit and began to cry with the agony.

'You're not eating,' shouted Daddy over my sobs, his face inches from mine. 'Better get started or I'll give you something to really cry about.

The pain in my hand was already almost more than I could bear. 'Please don't hit me again, Daddy. It hurts so much,' I begged.

'Well, you know what to do about it,' he told me calmly. 'Eat your tea.'

I looked at the scrap which still hung from the end of my fork and I swallowed hard, willing myself to eat the offending morsel. But I still couldn't do it. I knew I would be sick the moment it touched my tongue.

Daddy raised the baton again and I cringed in my seat waiting for another blow to my head or arms. I just hoped that it would knock me out so it would all be over with.

But he still had some surprises. He reached out his left hand and tore off a corner of one of the brawn slices on my plate, and pressed it on the rounded end of his baton. There was enough fat and jelly to make it stick there quite easily.

'Open wide, you little bastard,' he told me. 'You're going to eat this if I have to smash all your teeth to do it.'

By this time the pain and the panic combined were so much that I was no longer in control. I sat there, my body frozen, my mind seized up, unable to decide what to do.

Daddy decided for me. He suddenly stretched out his left hand and clamped his thumb and fingers over the end of my nose, squeezing it tightly. My mouth opened automatically as the air coming in through my nose was cut off, and Daddy pressed the end of his baton between my lips.

It was barred by my teeth, so he barked, 'Open wide or I'll knock your teeth down your throat, so help me.'

I was struggling to breathe and cry at the same time as little air was getting around the edge of the baton, and I opened my mouth as wide as it would go.

Daddy pushed the baton forward until its tip, with its covering of brawn, rammed against the back of my throat, stopping any air from getting in at all. I grabbed his left hand in both of mine and tried to prise his fingers off my nose.

At first he laughed. But I suppose he must finally have realised that he was choking me. Perhaps my face had turned bright red, because he suddenly released his grip on my nose and I was able to draw in some air.

But it was not enough. The baton had pushed back my tongue, and this and the brawn were now clogging my throat. I pushed against the table with both hands and finally my chair fell backwards and I followed it down, landing on my back with my head banging on the floor. But at least I had got free of the baton.

I spluttered and coughed and the piece of brawn shot out of my mouth as if from a catapult. My tongue felt swollen and sore and seemed to half-fill my mouth, and one of my teeth felt shaky.

All I could do was lie there on my back and suck in deep breaths in between sobs. I felt I had come very close to dying.

But Daddy hadn't quite finished with me yet. My bare legs were up in the air still, horizontal to the floor and hooked over the front of the fallen chair.

He walked around the table and glared down at me. 'You don't seem to realise. This is for your own damned good,' he told me, then he hit me hard with his baton twice, across my shins, just below my knees.

I couldn't help it. I screamed so hard that I wet myself again. I had no control left at all, the pain was so awful. I began to whimper and at that moment I hated my father more than anything else in the world, and wanted him dead.

'I hate you,' I managed to gasp between sobs.

Daddy sneered at me. 'And I hate you, you useless little bastard,' he said, and grabbed me by the hair and hauled me to my feet. It felt, for a moment, as though he was going to pull off my scalp.

Then Daddy slapped me a final time, hard, across my face. 'Get out of the house,' he yelled. 'I don't want to see you. Get out.'

I half-stumbled, half-fell down the stairs and through the shop below, hoping to find a comforting pair of arms and someone to kiss away my pain.

But Mammy was sitting behind the counter, apparently asleep. If she knew what had been happening upstairs she never made a sign, though I was pretty certain she had chosen to escape into her drug world again rather than cope with yet another family drama. These days she was rarely there when I needed her most.

I was still crying and hurting badly from the blows to my head, legs and hand and was desperately in need of warmth and tenderness. I knew there was none to be had at home, so I went in search of comfort, out through our back yard and along the lane.

Two doors down was the home of a playmate whose mother, Betty, had always had a few words of kindness and the odd hug for me, and I made my way through their yard, which like ours backed on to the lane.

When I walked through their back door, she took one look at me and gave a little cry of horror as she rushed forward and scooped me up in her arms. 'Oh, God, Michael. What has that monster done to you now?' she wailed.

'I fell downstairs again,' I sobbed. 'That's what happened. I fell downstairs again.'

'Hush, my darling,' she soothed, and sat down and began rocking me in her arms like a baby.

'I'm sorry, I've wet myself,' I sobbed.

She just hugged me closer and whispered, 'That doesn't matter, lovey. That doesn't matter.'

I felt that, with her as my mother, Daddy would never have dared to hit me. But, instead of a proper mammy, I now had an almost permanent zombie as a parent, and I knew in my heart that somehow that would have to do.

For just a while longer, I snuggled closer into Betty's arms and allowed myself to escape to a fantasy world where I was being cuddled and comforted by a loving, caring mother of my own.

Chapter Twelve

When I returned home that night, my legs and hand still throbbed with pain but our neighbour had replaced my damp trousers with a pair of her son's and my spirits had been almost restored by her cuddles and kindness.

They plummeted again, though, when I discovered that Daddy was still there, in the living room, watching television.

Mammy had made it upstairs by this time and was slumped next to him on the sofa, apparently asleep.

I nearly started to sob again, because I didn't think I could cope with another beating. There was only so much hurt I could stand.

But Daddy's mood had undergone one of its mercurial

changes and he greeted me, if not with a smile, at least not with anger on his face. He pointed towards the bedroom and told me, 'Get yourself off to bed, Michael. I'll be with you shortly.'

I knew then that I was not to be allowed the easy escape of curling up for sleep in my chair. Daddy was going to make me do that thing for him again.

I couldn't explain why, but each time he made me handle his willy I felt more and more revolted by what I was doing. I knew that what we were doing was wrong, because it felt wrong. I instinctively knew that I daren't breathe a word about it to another living soul, especially not my poor mother. I was too terrified by what he might do.

As soon as I was undressed, I slid between the sheets and lay there shivering, partly because it was cold and there was only one thin blanket, but also because I was very afraid, as I always was before these sessions in Daddy's bed.

That night he didn't give me time to fall asleep before he came to bed. Even with the bedclothes over my head, I heard him come in and undress, and then felt him slide into bed next to me.

I knew it was useless pretending to be asleep, because he would just go on shaking me until I responded, but I resolved not to make it easy for him. I wouldn't do anything, I told myself, until he made me. The wait wasn't long. He shook my shoulder and, in that special voice he always used on these occasions, said, 'Come on, Michael, you know what to do. Get on with it.'

The fact that he had savagely beaten me only a few hours earlier didn't seem to make the slightest difference to him. It was as though I was dealing with two completely separate daddies.

What he wanted me to do to him was a very intimate act – yet there was no real intimacy between us at all; we were like strangers.

'I can't do it,' I told him. 'My hand is all swollen and stiff where you bashed it with your baton. I can hardly use my fingers.'

'Then you'll have to use your other hand,' he said. 'So get on with it. And don't stop until I tell you to.'

I had to do it. There was never any winning with Daddy. He always made things go his way in the end. I started to cry, but I was determined he shouldn't know, and I held in my sobs while I did what he wanted.

As soon as it was over, I dried my hand on the sheet, away from me, and rolled on to my side, as far from Daddy as I could get. I was still crying when I fell asleep.

The next morning he was gone before I awoke.

It was another cold and dismal Manchester day and Mammy was still asleep on the sofa when I went downstairs, as usual, to forage in the shop for food.

I found an apple and a few wholemeal biscuits in an opened packet, and that was my breakfast. Two slices of stale bread, a few scraps of ham and an overripe banana were all I could find for my lunchbox, but, as so often happened, they would have to do.

When I shook Mammy's shoulder before leaving for

school, she actually opened her eyes and seemed to recognise me. But that was all. 'Home from school already, Michael?' she said.

'No, Mammy, I'm just going,' I told her, but got no sign that she had understood. But then I hadn't expected any.

She should have been opening the shop by now, but these days she was nearly always late. Another cause of frequent rows with Daddy, who claimed it was losing money.

Sometimes she was so late opening that she missed deliveries and was unable to make sandwiches for her regular customers, who were gradually turning to other, more reliable sources for their midday meals.

'It's time to open the shop,' I told her.

'In a minute,' she replied, closing her eyes again. 'In a minute. I'm awake now.'

I knew that, when Mammy said 'in a minute', it could mean anything, even the rest of the day, and that it was hopeless to go on trying to rouse her. How could a six-year-old succeed if a grown-up didn't want to co-operate?

On top of which I had my own problems to cope with. My hand was twice its normal size and dark blue and purple where Daddy had hit me with his baton. I had bathed it in cold water, which had sometimes helped in the past, but that didn't appear to have had any effect this time. It was still terribly painful and I could barely move my fingers, which were the size of little sausages.

My class teacher spotted it straight away and called me to the front. 'What have you done to your hand, Michael?'

'I shut it in a door,' I told her, having anticipated her interest and worked out a story on my walk to school.

By the look on her face, I don't think she believed me. Then she spotted the bruises on my shins and quickly covered her mouth with her hand. She seemed really shocked. 'What about your legs?' she asked. 'Don't tell me you got those bruises from a slammed door as well.'

'No, I didn't,' I said. 'I ran into a bench in the yard playing football.'

She shook her head. 'No one can be as clumsy as you claim to be,' she told me. 'I think a doctor needs to see that hand and then we can decide who else to call in.'

A part-time teacher was summoned to take me to the local hospital, where they X-rayed my hand.

'There's nothing broken. It's just badly bruised,' the doctor told her. 'But I would have expected the edge of a door to have left a scrape mark. This looks more like it received a blow from on top.'

'It was the door,' I told him. 'I slammed it and still had my hand around the edge.'

By the age of six I was so used to lying to cover up for Daddy's brutal attacks that I could look an adult straight in the eye when I explained my fantasy accidents.

'I suppose it might have happened that way,' the doctor told the teacher. 'It would be very hard to prove otherwise.'

And that seemed to be the end of it.

A nurse smeared ointment on my hand and bandaged it, then I was taken back to school.

After all the lies I had told that day to account for my bruises, it was a relief to be able to tell at least one person the truth.

'Daddy hit me with his baton,' I told Mammy when I got home and she asked about my bandaged hand.

'Does it hurt?' she asked.

'Yes, a lot.'

'I'll try to get him to stop,' she said. But she looked straight through me and I knew that she no longer had the spirit to fight with Daddy. To Mammy I had become a lost cause. It wasn't that she no longer cared, I don't think. It was simply that she was defeated, worn down by the screaming and the beatings and the hatred. That and the pills had taken away her ability to resist, her courage and even her will to survive.

At times likes this, I would pretend to myself that I lived with a normal family who loved me and with whom I was safe. It was the only way I could prevent myself from crying.

Mammy couldn't help me and neither could my teachers or the neighbours.

I was completely on my own and would have to find the strength inside myself to carry on.

Chapter Thirteen

Shortly after my seventh birthday, in June 1964, Mammy told me that we were to leave Manchester – for good.

For months now, the bulldozers had been at work along the Ashton Old Road, demolishing the houses. By June, they were only a block away from us and Mammy said the council had told us we had to leave by the end of August.

Daddy had also been told that he was no longer needed at Strangeways and would have to find a new job. Later, I heard it was something to do with his treatment of a prisoner but I never discovered the whole story.

For weeks, whenever Mammy was lucid enough, which was less and less often, all they seemed to talk about was money – and our lack of it. We couldn't afford to buy a home and from what I understood neither could we afford to live in another council property – even if one was offered in a decent part of Manchester. The only solution was to move in with one or other of my grandmothers. For me, that meant a choice between salvation and utter disaster.

As the time for us to move drew closer and the rows between Mammy and Daddy became almost continuous, so did my beatings. I was punched and slapped and kicked almost every day and had so many cuts and bruises I would never have been able to explain them at school.

But it was the summer holidays and, apart from two of our neighbours, there was nobody who seemed to care what happened to me.

Mammy no longer made any attempt to shield me or even comfort me after a thrashing. She had once again became a regular target for Daddy's brutality and was barely able to cope with her own injuries, let alone mine. I knew it wasn't personal. It wasn't that she didn't care about me. She didn't care about anything any more.

Every moment Daddy was at home I spent in a state of high anxiety. I knew that he was going to bash me at some point, but I didn't know when and I didn't know what form his attack would take. Sometimes I became so frightened, waiting for the beating, that I would wet myself. I knew that at times I smelled because of it, but this was a very small worry compared with my main concern – guessing how the next lot of pain would be inflicted. The anticipation of what was to come was often far worse than the beating itself.

One thing that didn't change was his demands for my services in his bed. The milking may have given Daddy some kind of satisfaction, but my efforts never earned a word of gratitude or reduced the brutality of his attacks.

Daddy no longer wore his black prison uniform and I understood that he had started work with the telephone company. I think he hated giving up the uniform and that is why he was so bad-tempered all the time. But I was pleased because it meant he had also given up his baton, which was the thing I feared most when he attacked me.

One day in early August, Mammy told me that they had decided to move in with her mother and father in Bolton. I experienced a sudden surge of hope – even happiness. Nanny Ramsden was the only person in the family who had ever shown me any real love.

She was big and jolly and kind and cheerful. Living with her had to be better than my life so far in Manchester, where I was dependent for everything on a brutal and sadistic father and a drug-addicted mother.

Thank God, they had not chosen to live with my other grandmother. I remembered staying with Grandma Seed only once and it had been a very unpleasant few days. She obviously hated Mammy and looked at me as though I was not a boy but a piece of dirt that someone had brought in on their shoe. She was a sour-faced, bitter and demanding old woman and Mammy and I had secretly nicknamed her 'the Wicked Witch of the West'.

When the day came for us to leave the Ashton Old Road, the bulldozers were only three doors away and the whole area was like the bombsites that had been boarded up by the council. It was rumoured that a huge new supermarket was to be built on the land where our house now stood, but at the time I didn't know what that meant.

We drove to Bolton in Daddy's old banger. The light-blue Ford Anglia, with its horrible cheap plastic seats, narrow bonnet, big front mudguards and frog-eye headlights, belched out clouds of smoke all the way.

We took only our clothes, some bedding, the television set and a few ornaments and trinkets. All our furniture was left behind. The shop had been stripped of all its goods the week before by a man who ran a similar shop in another part of Manchester. When we left, Daddy didn't even bother to close the door. A thief would have to be pretty desperate to take any of the stuff we were leaving behind, he said.

None of us looked back when we drove away. I think it was a relief for everyone to be going. As far back as I could remember, there had been only unhappiness there. For Mammy and Daddy and for me.

Things could only get better in our new home, I told myself, and I willed it to be so.

I couldn't have been more horribly wrong.

PART TWO

PART TWO

Chapter Fourteen

The journey to hell takes exactly 39 minutes and is made in total silence.

That is the time it took us to get to Nanny and Granddad Ramsden's house in Bolton, on the north-west edge of Greater Manchester — the place where I was destined to confront my personal hell on earth.

Neither of my parents spoke a word during the 11-mile drive — Mammy because she had taken her usual quota of pills that morning and was in her customary limbo; and Daddy because he rarely ever spoke when he was behind the wheel.

I sat in the back, with my knees under my chin, hugging my legs and wondering what effect this change in our family fortunes was going to have on me. I couldn't guess what kind of school I would go to, or what the children I would meet there would be like, but I did dare to hope that, with my lovely Nanny Ramsden to protect me, I would no longer be a victim of Daddy's brutality.

I had seen my grandparents only on rare visits to Bolton and we had never stayed more than a few hours, usually for a tea of tinned salmon — which, perversely, despite my loathing for fish, I quite liked — in sandwiches with salad cream.

Granddad Ramsden was called Joseph, like my father, and that made me suspect that all men baptised with that name were the same — mean-spirited, bad-tempered and full of hatred for small boys.

He was a grumpy, unsmiling old man, who spent most of his waking hours in a high-backed wooden chair by the fire, either issuing Nanny with petty orders or complaining about everyone and everything to anyone who would listen and sometimes even if no one was there.

A retired miner, he usually dressed in an old-fashioned shirt with no collar and did not bother to shave regularly. I sometimes saw him in the bath or washing in the kitchen sink, stripped to the waist, and his back was covered with shingles. They itched like mad, Nanny told me, and probably were much to blame for his bad temper.

Nanny had been a weaver when she met Granddad, but had given up work after Mammy was born. They had moved into their council house in 1935, when it was brand new, and had later adopted a 14-year-old boy, my uncle Leslie. He had left home to join the RAF years before we moved in, and was himself married. Sadly, we rarely met when I was a boy, but later I discovered that Leslie was a kind and decent man.

From the very first day we moved in, Granddad bluntly let it be known that he was not happy having us there. He complained, long and loudly, that the house was far too cramped and tiny for the five of us, and that by moving in we had selfishly, and unforgivably, disrupted his life. He made it blatantly obvious to everyone from the moment we arrived that he hated us being there and wanted rid of us.

From the start, it was difficult to know which of the two of us he disliked most, my father or myself. He never had a kind word or a smile for either of us, and I know that Daddy loathed his being top dog in the house. They fought verbally often and loudly, and twice came to blows, with Granddad, surprisingly and to my secret delight, getting the better of Daddy.

That first day, when I dared to think that a peaceful home life was still possible, saw the first of their rows; and, as so often would be the case, it was about me.

There was no question that the place was small. It was a typical, cheaply and shoddily built, two-up and two-down council house. At the front there was a living-cum-dining room, at the back a kitchen and upstairs two bedrooms and a toilet.

My first question to Nanny had been to ask where my room would be, and she had patiently explained that I would be sharing a room with Mammy and Daddy, sleeping on a little bed in the corner. It was probably stupid of me to have imagined otherwise, but somehow I had assumed that, when we moved, for the first time in my life I would get a room of my very own.

My disappointment must have been painted clearly on my face, and obvious to everyone, because my father lashed out with the back of his hand and whacked me hard on the side of my head.

'Wipe that expression of your face,' he snarled. 'You should be grateful you're getting a place to sleep anywhere.'

That's when Granddad exploded. 'Don't you go bloody bashing people in my house, Joe Seed,' he bellowed. 'I'm the master of this bloody house, and me and only me'll decide when some bugger needs a thrashing, not you. Do you understand?'

'I'll give my boy a seeing-to whenever I feel like it,' my father shouted just as loudly.

'But not in my bloody house you won't,' growled Granddad. 'And if you don't bloody like it then you can just pack up your things again and get out now. Nothing would please me more.'

I think I could be excused for having assumed at this point that Granddad had interfered in order to protect me. At least that's what I thought at the time, and so I sidled over towards where he was sitting, believing I would be safer there.

A sudden backhander across my face from him quickly changed my mind. And, if this violent blow wasn't enough to disillusion me, his words quickly left me in no doubt as to where he stood.

'Don't expect any bloody sympathy from me, you little tyke. You probably deserve your arse being kicked. But in this house it's me who does the kicking. No one else.' And he glared at Daddy, then down at me.

In just five minutes, all my hopes for an easier existence had been destroyed and I had been reduced, as so often happened in my life, to a sobbing, pathetic heap on the floor.

Neither Mammy nor Nanny had done a thing to defend me from either of the men during their outburst of anger, and I knew right then, at the very beginning of our stay in Bolton, that there was going to be no protection at all for me in that house.

I think Nanny was as frightened of Granddad as Mammy was of Daddy, and it made me suspect that she too was used to receiving a beating.

I still wonder to this day what on earth had possessed my mother to make her marry a carbon copy of her father. She must have seen her own mother undergo suffering similar to her own on countless occasions.

So, nothing had changed; except that I could now look forward to being pounced on and beaten by *two* vicious, angry old men instead of just one.

It was clear to all of us from the outset that Daddy and Granddad detested each other with equal ferocity. They took great pains to avoid any more contact than was absolutely necessary, even to the point, or so everyone said behind his back, that Daddy deliberately arranged to work mostly nights in his new job as a supervisor at the telephone exchange. That way, he spent most of his days sleeping and we saw little of him.

In her parents' house, Mammy was expected to sleep in the marital bed and could no longer avoid sharing it with Daddy by sleeping in a chair. It also meant, to my great delight, that Daddy could no longer force me into his bed to take part in the unpleasant milking sessions, and on the nights he was out working, Mammy, when she was conscious enough to remember, would suggest that I share the big bed with her, to be more comfortable.

Our room looked out on to our back garden and, beyond a dirt path, to a big area of allotments and then open scrubland.

Nanny and Granddad slept in the front bedroom, which was slightly bigger, and between the two bedrooms was the toilet. This was enlarged by the council after we had been there a few months, to make room for a fitted bath. But initially bath night still involved a tin tub in front of the kitchen fire.

The house, number seven, was one of dozens of identical houses in Raikes Road, a cul-de-sac that ran downhill to end in a huge area of wasteground which I soon discovered the local kids called 'No Man's Land'.

That's where I learned to run to when I saw trouble brewing at home. I would use the excuse of walking Nanny's dog, an old golden Labrador called Sophie; she had been rejected as a guide dog by the local school for the blind and would turn out to prove a better friend than most people I met in Bolton.

The suburb of Darcy Lever, where we lived, appeared to be one vast council estate. But Nanny's attitude certainly didn't reflect this, for she was as house-proud as though she lived in the poshest of areas. Every Saturday morning, she polished the furniture to a high sheen and the house always smelled of Johnson's wax. There was a big sideboard in the front room with glassware in it and a china tea service which was never used.

Nanny loved green. She had a dark-green fitted carpet in the front room, which had dark-green and white wallpaper. That was the colour scheme in Nanny's bedroom as well, while our bedroom had light-green and white wallpaper. When it came to the kitchen they must have run out of green paint. The walls were white and there were home-made scatter rugs on the flagstone floor.

Nanny also prided herself on never being a penny in debt. When the rent man came, every Thursday afternoon, she would always be waiting on the doorstep to pay him in cash.

Three houses uphill Raikes Road crossed the bus route into the centre of Bolton, which lay about three-quarters of a mile to the north-west, to become Long Lane, and this ran north all the way to the Bury Road, with the great expanse of Leverhulme Park on its left.

Just before this junction with the Bury Road, my new school was sited, next to a Catholic church which bore the same name: St Osmund's. Walking to school along Long Lane, and just a hundred yards from our house, you crossed over a brick railway bridge, under which the Bolton to Bury trains ran through a deep cutting.

I didn't know it then but that bridge and that gully were to feature in my nightmares for many years – and still do on rare occasions. The track has long since been removed, but at that time trains passed by there several times a day, and to me were still objects of interest rather than horror.

In the Ramsden house, I quickly established that the kitchen was the friendliest and safest place for me to be. It was away from Granddad, in his chair in the living room, and close to Nanny, who spent most of her waking hours there, creating wonderful dishes, such as steak and kidney pudding and jam roly-poly and custard.

After years of existing on sandwiches and fruit and rarely having tasted a hot meal, I was in seventh heaven. At least my stomach was.

The house always smelled of cooking, often of fish, which Nanny loved and I loathed, and of chicken soup, another of her favourites. She listened to the radio while she worked and never missed *Woman's Hour* and *The Archers*. Away from the kitchen, she was a great fan of *Coronation Street and Z Cars on the television.*

Nanny's cooking always tasted marvellous and there was lots of it. Breakfast was there waiting for me every morning before I went to school, and a wonderful hot meal greeted me when I came home.

Nanny was a large, cuddly woman who, although quite strict and a stickler for cleanliness and good manners, also liked to laugh, and generally, at least at first, she was cheerful when we were alone. I loved it when there were just the two of us, because she would tell me stories about her life and about Mammy as a girl and young woman. They were usually funny tales about trivial events, but sometimes they became quite serious.

It was during these one-to-one sessions with Nanny that I learned how my parents had met. Mammy had been sent up to a place near Blackpool to work in a wartime armaments factory, and it was there that she had met my father, who was a bomber navigator in the RAF.

Joe Seed had served throughout the war and had been on some of the most famous bomber raids on Germany. Sometimes, during the rare moments Daddy spent with us downstairs, Nanny would get him to reminisce about the mysterious war years. From the animated way he talked and even laughed, I gathered they were the happiest years of his life, though at the time I understood little about the stories he was telling.

Nanny also talked to me about Mammy's childhood sweetheart, Harold Orton, though never when Daddy was there. There was a Salvation Army citadel in Darcy Lever where Harold was a handsome and dashing lieutenant. In those days, Nanny and Granddad were still devout Salvation Army members and Granddad even played a trumpet in the brass band. Nanny often sighed when she told me how much she regretted Mammy leaving home and falling in love with Daddy.

'It was a wartime infatuation and nothing more, and that's what it should have remained,' she told me on many occasions. 'Lillian and Harold were meant for each other. She should have married him. I like your Daddy, Michael, but I think my Lillian would have been much happier with Harold.' Then she would sigh again and sometimes take out a tissue and wipe her eyes.

Harold remained a friend of my grandparents for many years and would often visit them. Eventually, he had married a lovely American lady whom he met through the Salvation Army, and he rose to become Deputy Commander of the whole international movement.

I met Harold again when I was much older and, probably because of his former fondness for my mother, we developed a lasting friendship.

Even though I was only seven years old when I first heard these stories, I grasped that Mammy might well have been a lot happier had she stayed in Bolton and married her sweetheart, and that Nanny would certainly have been a much more contented parent.

The Seed family may have loathed their son marrying a non-Catholic working-class girl, but Nanny Ramsden had been equally opposed to the match. She was deeply shocked when her daughter chose one of the despised papists, as she then considered him, for a husband and, worse, Mammy actually adopted his hated religion in order to marry him.

I didn't know what religion was in those days, so a lot of Nanny's stories went over my head, but I enjoyed going with her to Salvation Army meetings. The people there were always very kind and nice to me and I loved the brass bands.

Soon after I started my new Catholic primary school, however, I was ordered by the resident priest to join the church choir and this drew some very dark looks from Nanny.

'That damned priest is just seeking a way to sneak in here and preach at us for being Salvationists,' was her reaction, and she may have been right, for on several occasions the priest called at our house to talk to my parents, he said, about my spiritual welfare.

Mammy and Daddy were never available when he called, so he got Nanny and Granddad instead. Well, Nanny really, because Granddad just stared straight through him as though he wasn't there, and never spoke. Nanny wasn't the least bit intimidated by the priest's dog collar and gave him a verbal trouncing whenever he questioned her allegiance to the Salvation Army.

'God doesn't need idolatry to mark the path to heaven,' she would lecture him, and eventually he stopped coming to the house.

Even so, the priest wanted me to attend the Catholic church on Sunday mornings and choir practice midweek, and needless to say I had to go on my own. If I did miss a Mass for some reason, I would always pay dearly for it on Monday morning, when he would cane every child who had skipped church on Sunday. And, if I mentioned that I had been to a Salvation Army meeting instead, he would become noticeably more angry and give me a second thrashing on my backside.

Strangely enough, I loved the mystery of the Catholic Mass, which was all said in Latin in those days, though it was much more fun going to Salvation Army meetings.

Only the priest and Nanny seemed concerned about my spiritual welfare. My parents didn't care less which church I attended on Sundays, or even if I went to one at all.

Before my first day at St Osmund's School, I had been nervous and frightened. I knew that the teachers and children would all be strangers, which was bad enough, but it also worried me that I couldn't do any of the normal things in school, like read, write or do sums. I'd expected that all the other kids would make fun of me, as they had done in Manchester.

It didn't surprise me at all when my parents made feeble excuses not to take me to school on my first day, and I resigned myself to getting there alone. But Nanny would have none of it. From that moment, as she did for the next ten years, she took responsibility for my upbringing – and because of that I loved her unreservedly in return. Without her strength and kindness, I would never have survived.

It was she who volunteered to accompany me on the mile walk to school at the far end of Long Lane, and on the way even introduced me to some of her neighbours' children so that I would have someone to talk to and walk with on the journey to and from school in the years to come.

I can see now that even back then Nanny had recognised that my mother was no longer capable of being a proper parent and was already standing in for her. Between them, Mammy's husband and father were gradually obliterating my mother as a person.

On that first day, as she did every day for the rest of my time at school, Nanny had carefully prepared a snack, a first for me; and, remembering that I didn't drink milk, she also tucked a bottle of orange juice into my satchel.

At St Osmund's, Nanny walked me through the playground and into school, and introduced me to the headmaster, Mr Bleasdale, who would prove another great source of strength and encouragement in the future.

As I had feared, it didn't take my teachers or the other kids long to realise how backward I was. I couldn't do anything. I don't know why, but I didn't want to learn. Nothing went into my brain. Nothing written on the blackboard made any sense to me and I never did learn to do the simplest of arithmetic. But, surprisingly, my teachers still put no real pressure on me, even at seven. There was a long way to go, they said, before the 11-plus, and they hoped there would be a marked improvement in my ability, or at least my will to learn, long before then.

Recognising my multiple deficiencies in academic and social skills, the other children soon labelled me the school dunce. This made me an instant figure of fun in the playground, someone to be teased and pointed and laughed at, the butt of a dozen daily jokes and pranks. It wasn't easy to cope with, though it was no worse than I had expected. I was uneducated but I wasn't stupid.

Very few boys, except for some of those introduced to me by Nanny, wanted to be friends and play with me, but I didn't care. I was used to being a loner, and already conditioned, I suppose, to being ignored or disliked by others.

Besides, the situation at home was deteriorating again and that provided me with more than enough worries to occupy my mind and my time. Almost immediately after our arrival in Bolton, Mammy had started to act even more strangely than before. Poor Mammy, I think she was still trying to run away – but had nowhere to go. She would leave home early in the morning and stay away until late at night, and would never talk to anyone about where she had been. This made Nanny very unhappy.

I would sometimes find her in tears when I came home from school, and then she would talk to me about her fears. Though just a child of seven, I was the only person in the house she could talk to about it. Granddad and Daddy chose to ignore the fact that Mammy was missing for most of the time, and that, when she was at home, she was so drugged she never made any kind of sense when she did speak.

'Your mammy is very unwell, Michael,' Nanny would say to me. 'I really don't know what's going to happen to her. It breaks my heart that she doesn't feel she has anything to live for. It's Joe Seed who has been her ruin. The only way she'll ever be herself again is if she gets shut of him. But it's gone beyond that, I think.'

I could see that getting rid of Daddy would make both Mammy and me much happier, but I didn't understand an awful lot of what Nanny was confiding in me. What I remember most is that she was a comforting pair of arms to go to after I had been attacked by either Daddy or Granddad, though only if she happened to be in another room. She would never try to protect or comfort me in front of the men, no matter how badly they beat me, and I never blamed her for this. Instinctively, I knew that she was frightened of causing the same brutal aggression to be directed against herself should she intervene in any way.

Granddad's initial warning to Daddy did not deter him in the slightest. He certainly didn't stop his attacks on me or on Mammy. They were less frequent, but in no way less violent than before, but now they went on almost exclusively in the privacy of our bedroom. Of course, this didn't mean that they remained secret, because time and again we bore the marks of Daddy's assaults.

I understood Nanny's reasons for not interfering, and I think Granddad's policy must have been that, as long as he pretended he didn't hear anything, he didn't have to do anything. Either way, it meant that Mammy and I were still constantly vulnerable and often on the receiving end of a great deal of pain.

Sometimes Daddy would come into our room angry when we were in bed and drag us from under the bedclothes and begin pounding us with his fists while we were still half-asleep. It was a terrifying way to be forced awake – to feel the dreadful pain but momentarily not know where it was coming from.

Even worse for me was to realise that Mammy no longer offered any resistance at all; that she had completely given in. She would just let herself be hit until she was knocked over. When Daddy punched her, she no longer screamed but just moaned and didn't try at all to stop him. It became much harder for me to witness her beatings than before, because I could remember how at one time she used to fight back or at least tried to dodge the blows. But now, after she was knocked down, she would lie there sobbing until she went back to the welcome cure-all of sleep.

My grandparents could not have been unaware of this brutality going on under their roof, but almost invariably they chose to ignore it. So the noise of our beatings was never mentioned, until one morning, after a particularly savage attack, when Mammy came down to breakfast with a black eye, cuts on her cheek and lip and a swollen jaw. I was in little better shape. My face was bruised and swollen in several places, though I had not been cut.

Granddad scowled but didn't say a word, even after Daddy came in. He just stood up and hit Daddy on the point of his jaw with his right fist, very hard.

I don't know whether it was the force of the blow, or

the surprise, but Daddy went down backwards, hard on to his bottom, and sat there looking stunned. I heard Nanny's loud gasp from across the room.

'I warned you about who's the master in this house, Joe Seed,' Granddad said angrily. 'So you can bloody well get yourself out of here – now – and I don't want to see you back.'

Mammy and I looked at Granddad, then at each other and then at Daddy, who was clambering to his feet. I think we both expected an explosion. But Daddy simply went upstairs to get his jacket and then walked out of the house without saying a word.

I heard later that he had gone to stay with his mother in Halewood, a suburb of Liverpool. A week later, he was back in Bolton. I don't know how it was arranged or who negotiated the truce between Daddy and Granddad, but he suddenly appeared again one night, and nothing was said.

It was a big disappointment for me, and I imagine for Mammy as well. I had really believed that our days of being terrorised by Daddy were over; and that if I could steer clear of Granddad those vicious attacks were a thing of the past.

But nothing in my life was ever going to prove quite that easy.

Chapter Fifteen

The beating which caused Granddad to throw Daddy out of the house was also responsible for bringing social workers to our new home.

My class teacher at St Osmund's and the headmaster did not believe my story that the bruises on my face were caused by a tumble downstairs. Mr Bleasdale repeatedly demanded to know who had attacked me and, in the end, in desperation, I told him I had been waylaid by a gang of older boys on my way home from school the previous evening and it was they who had inflicted the injuries to my face.

At this point, I squeezed out a few tears and sobs and told them I had been frightened to speak until now because the boys had threatened to hurt me even more if I told on them.

I could see that Mr Bleasdale still wasn't fully convinced I was telling the truth, but this time I stuck to my story. It was just unthinkable that I could disclose that it was Daddy who had battered me, because retribution from him would have been ten times worse than from any gang of yobs.

Eventually, the headmaster gave up asking questions, though he warned me that he intended to investigate further and that someone from the social services would be calling at my home.

When two child-welfare officers, a man and a woman, turned up three days later, I had already passed on to Nanny the details of the story I had concocted for Mr Bleasdale. Nanny explained that only she, Granddad, Mammy and I lived there. It wasn't a complete lie, because Daddy was at that time still conforming to Granddad's order and living elsewhere. She and Granddad swore that no one had been ill-treating me, while Mammy dumbly nodded her agreement. I'm not certain that she even understood who the visitors were, and oddly they never questioned her about the damage Daddy had done to her face.

Granddad told them gruffly that he occasionally clipped me round the ear for being naughty, but never hard enough to cause any real injuries. What a whopper that was.

Then he and Nanny complained about the young hooligans terrorising the estate and inflicting pain and misery on the younger children. I was astonished at the way they embellished my original lie, adding the kind of details I could never have thought of.

Seemingly having run out of questions, the social workers finally went away – still suspicious, I'm sure, but lacking any evidence to pursue the matter further.

I was so certain that, even if they had known the truth, they could not have stopped my father or my grandfather from beating me. It never occurred to me that they could have taken me away and placed me in care for my own protection. Had that option been explained to me, I would have confessed everything in an instant. Only a complete fool would have chosen to go on taking the kind of regular punishment I was receiving rather than seek safe alternative accommodation. I knew that no threats or warnings from the authorities would have influenced those two men. They were bullies, both of them, and far too angry and mean to change their ways; especially since I was a convenient and easy victim, too weak and too small to fight back. And now Mammy had become the same.

Even so, after witnessing all those unsuccessful attempts she had made to kill herself with pills, I suppose I had come to believe that Mammy was indestructible and would always come back from the edge of the grave at the very last moment. And that is why, I think now, it was doubly shattering for me, at eight years of age, that, after talking about it for so many years, she had finally found a way to escape her tormentor for ever. Having chosen a more reliable method than pills, she at last succeeded in killing herself. But, in escaping from Daddy, she abandoned me.

She did it on a March morning in 1966, though it was to be days before I learned the full details of what had happened.

Normally on a Saturday morning, I would have been at the kids' club in the Odeon cinema, Bolton, and Granddad, who was a part-time lollipop man, would have been supervising the children crossing the road outside the picture palace. Because of his job, he could get me in free. We would walk the mile from our house to the cinema together and sometimes he would ask me to carry his 'Children Crossing' sign.

But on that particular Saturday morning, for some reason I can no longer remember, we had not gone to Bolton. Instead, I was in the kitchen chatting with Nanny when a neighbour banged on the back door and then rushed in without waiting for an answer. She was very excited and panting and red in the face, from running I think; her eyes were big and round and she was clasping her hands together.

She just stood there in the doorway for a few moments, then blurted out to Nanny, 'It's poor Lillian, Polly. You have to come quickly.'

I thought it odd that someone should so urgently want Nanny to go and see my Mammy, who had gone out early that morning before I was up, as she so often did, probably heading for the secret hideaway where she had been spending so many of her days of late. She hadn't said goodbye and that was not unusual either. But it was to become terribly important to me when I was told what she had done. I just couldn't accept that Mammy would choose to go away for ever without saying goodbye to me. If she really loved me, as she had said, how could she have abandoned me?

I think Nanny knew straight away what had happened. Suddenly, she looked as though she had had all the stuffing knocked out of her. At eight, you are fairly switched on to what is going on around you, and watching Nanny, whose ruddy cheeks had gone very pale, and who had started to shake all over, I could hardly miss that something very dramatic must have happened, and that it involved Mammy.

Our neighbour looked at me in a very odd way and then went over and whispered in Nanny's ear, which made her look even more unwell.

'Oh my God,' Nanny said very quietly, almost to herself, and then went into the living room, before reappearing a few seconds later with Granddad, who also looked shocked.

'Is Joe upstairs?' he asked, and I noticed that his voice was quaking.

Nanny nodded and he went to the bottom of the stairs and shouted, 'Joe, come down now. We think something terrible has happened to Lillian. You need to come with me, now, to find out what's up.'

My father was downstairs in a flash, and moments later

he and Granddad and the neighbour were gone without any of them saying another word.

By now I was very curious and more than a little apprehensive.

'What's happened to Mammy?' I asked Nanny. 'Is she all right? Is she coming home?'

'I don't really know, Michael,' she said. 'I think your Mammy may have had an accident. That's where Granddad and your daddy have gone. We'll just wait here until they come home.'

I began to feel very nervous and frightened. If Mammy had been in an accident, I thought, then she might be badly hurt.

'I ought to go and help her,' I said.

But when I tried to leave, Nanny grabbed my arm and held me back. 'Best to wait here, Michael,' she said. 'We don't know where she is at the moment. And Daddy will want you to be here when he gets back.'

It was ages before they did come home, but the moment they appeared in the doorway I knew something really terrible had happened. Daddy was crying, the tears streaming down his cheeks, and he did something that he had never done before. He came over to me and gathered me into his arms and hugged me close to him. It was the first time I could remember him ever giving me a hug, and I was filled with terror. I knew that for this to happen something absolutely dreadful must have occurred. To cause this change in Daddy, it had to be something very bad indeed.

He didn't even try to explain himself. He released me and went upstairs, pausing only to say to Nanny, 'You'd better tell him, Mum. It'll come better from you.'

By this time she was crying as well, and even Granddad had wet eyes. He looked quite horrified, as though he had been forced to look at something which nobody should be expected to see. His eyes were darting about all over the place and he was shaking worse than Nanny.

She came over and put her arms around me, as Daddy had done, and told me quietly that Mammy would not be coming home to us ever again – she had died in an accident.

Even when I heard the words, I couldn't take them in properly. They just weren't registering. I was stunned. It couldn't be true, I told her. It wasn't possible.

If you don't actually see the dead body of somebody you know very well, it is very difficult to believe it has happened. Had her death followed an overdose of pills, I could have accepted it more easily. But this didn't make sense. How could Mammy not be coming back – ever? I began to panic, and the tears started to flow.

Nanny just carried on hugging me and talking to me. 'I'm so sorry, Michael,' she said. 'I know she loved you so much, but now, however hard, we have to accept that she is gone. That she is in heaven now and has found the peace and happiness she has always wanted.'

It was then that I finally started to believe the unbelievable, and I think I went slightly crazy. I screamed and shouted and cried and dropped to the floor. I can remember punching the rug until my fists throbbed. I have never forgotten how angry I felt. Mammy had finally escaped, as she had always promised she would do one day, but she hadn't taken me with her. She had lied to me all along. It can't have been just Daddy she wanted to get away from. She obviously wanted to get away from me as well.

I was still sobbing on the floor when the police came to the house, and Nanny had to scoop me up and lead me into the living room while they all talked in the kitchen behind a closed door.

Later that afternoon, Nanny explained to me that Mammy had fallen on the railway tracks and been killed, but she didn't mention that it was suicide.

I did rack my brains, though, trying to work out how she had come to fall. I crossed the Long Lane railway bridge, the main one in Darcy Lever, every morning and every afternoon on my way to and from school, and it had a brick wall on either side which I could barely see over. It was much too tall for Mammy to have accidentally fallen over.

I was still puzzling about this when the time came for me to go to bed. When Daddy told me I should get into the big bed, I didn't think there was anything strange about that, as it was something Mammy had asked me to do so often.

I felt exhausted, but I couldn't get to sleep, still unable to come to terms with the fact that Mammy was dead. I was scared and bewildered just trying to envisage a future without her.

When Daddy came to bed, I was still awake but was taken totally by surprise when I felt his hand grip my wrist. Even if I'd been asleep it would have woken me. He shook me slightly and asked, 'Are you awake, Michael?'

I told him I was, and fully expected him to start talking to me about Mammy and the dreadful loss we must be sharing.

Instead, he remained silent and pulled my hand towards him until it touched his naked body. 'You know what to do,' he said in that strange voice I still remembered from the last time this had happened, over a year before, and which I had hoped never to hear again.

I was stunned for the second time that day. Only hours earlier, my life had been turned upside down. Mammy was dead and never coming home, and all Daddy wanted was for me to take part in that bizarre ritual of producing milk. In the past, I had found it distasteful, but suddenly, perhaps because of the circumstances, the whole idea had become utterly repugnant and I tried to pull my hand away.

But Daddy clung to my wrist and told me if I didn't do as I was told it would be the worse for me. I started to cry in earnest. I felt that my heart was actually breaking, and I had definitely never experienced such absolute sorrow in my life before. And all Daddy could do was to threaten to hurt me even more if I didn't perform that sickening act for him.

'Please don't make me. Not tonight,' I begged him through my sobs, but he gripped my wrist even harder and dug his nails into my flesh.

'Do it right now, or you'll regret it for the rest of your life, you little bastard,' he snarled, and in that moment I believed that he must have been waiting for Mammy to die, just so he could go back to indulging with me in this weird and repulsive practice.

I hated myself for doing it, on this night of all nights, but I eventually reached out and grabbed his willy, because I was too frightened to defy him any longer.

'That's better,' he said, and released his grip on my wrist as I began to stroke and rub him in the way he had taught me. He pushed the bedclothes down to his legs and in minutes he was gasping and sighing and I felt the warm liquid on my hand.

I wiped it on the sheet, knowing that now it was over he would have no further interest in me, and got out of bed and went to my own small bed in the corner, where I burrowed under the blankets and curled into a little ball until I fell asleep.

But on this night it wasn't over. I don't know how much later it was but I was woken by Daddy dragging me back into his bed again, where I was forced to go through the whole disgusting performance once more.

I can't remember ever being more unhappy, or desperate for love, than I was at that moment. I wanted so much to be with Mammy and out of Daddy's clutches for ever, and if that meant dying I would just have to kill myself, I decided.

Chapter Sixteen

The first time I heard that my mother had killed herself by jumping in front of a train was in the playground at school, from a bunch of eight-year-old boys and girls.

Even at that age, I thought I was capable of putting on a brave face and coping with anything life could throw at me, but this was the most awful episode I had encountered. It was more than a crisis. It was a catastrophe.

The children were extremely cruel, and the bullying and the name-calling so revolting that I came close to being physically sick. Every conceivable foul name was used to describe Mammy and me. It was the start of my crucifixion.

At first, my mind went completely numb. I just

couldn't accept what they were screeching at me: that Mammy had deliberately hurled herself from the bridge into the path of a train. They used words like 'splatter', 'mangled' and 'buckets of blood' and laughed about it. But it wasn't their mammy they were talking about. It was mine.

To them, it was just a juicy new titbit of information with which to punish the school dunce. To me, it was my whole life.

I couldn't hold back the tears, but crying in front of the other children didn't seem that important compared with the dreadfulness of the things I was hearing.

I kept shouting at them, 'It's not true. It's not true,' and they kept shouting, 'Yes it is. Yes it is. Your mother was mad and you're mad too.'

In the end, I lost all control and rushed at one of my worst tormentors, a ginger-haired boy in my class, who had always poked fun at me. I ran into him with such force that I knocked him over backwards and ended up sitting on his stomach and pummelling with my fists at his head and chest.

'You're lying,' I shouted. 'It's all lies.'

He flailed his arms in an effort to stop my blows connecting, and shouted back, 'It's not a lie. It was in yesterday's paper.'

Another voice yelled in my ear, 'My dad told us all about it, and he heard it straight from your dad, so it must be true.'

This was worse than awful. Why hadn't they told me

at home, where I could have let my grief come out in private? Why had they exposed me to this baiting from my fellow pupils? Why hadn't anyone cared enough to tell me the truth?

At that moment I went into complete withdrawal. I wanted to die right there and then. The only way forward that I could see was to copy what Mammy had done and kill myself. I could see no point in living at all.

She's shown me the escape route, I reasoned. Now all I need to do is take it and I'm free. It was a thought which was to stay with me every day for the next seven years, and on several occasions I looked death in the face from very close quarters in my determination to kill myself.

The next most difficult moment of that hellish day came on the way home. Mr Bleasdale had insisted on walking me home from school because he wanted, he said, to talk to my father and grandparents. I learned much later that they had sent me to school that day in the hope that thrusting me into my normal routine would provide the best therapy for me to cope with Mammy's death. They were hopelessly wrong, of course, and I think Mr Bleasdale had recognised their mistake and perhaps guessed what was in my mind – the thought of jumping off the same bridge from which Mammy had leaped to her death.

When we reached the middle of the bridge I stopped, and Mr Bleasdale took my arm.

'Is this where it happened? I asked him.

He nodded. 'Yes.'

I don't know what I expected to feel but all I could think about was that this was where Mammy had stood when she was last alive. I took a deep breath through my nose, knowing I was being crazy but hoping that I would smell her perfume or the scent of her lipstick or powder, anything that would bring her back to me, however fleetingly.

But of course there was nothing but the smell of the smoke from the coal fires of late winter. I think that is when I really accepted that Mammy wasn't coming back.

'She's gone for ever,' I told Mr Bleasdale

He nodded again. 'I'm afraid so, Michael,' he said, and we walked on.

I don't know what was said to Nanny and my father, but the next morning, instead of being sent to school, I was told by Daddy that he had arranged for me to go away for a few weeks. I didn't care. They had betrayed me by not telling me what had really happened. Right then, I hated them.

Daddy said a change of scenery would do me good. After my day at school, I thought so too. The other children had acted like monsters and I knew it was pointless to think they would let it drop after just one day. They had tasted blood and they would want more.

Then he told me he was driving me to his mother's home in Halewood and my heart sank. Oh no, this is not rescue, I thought.

I was being delivered directly into the hands of the Wicked Witch of the West.

Chapter Seventeen

The Wicked Witch was thin and bony and had a big nose, tiny squinty eyes and a thin rat-trap mouth. Even her laugh was cruel and, though she smelled of lavender, there was nothing sweet about her.

When we arrived at her bungalow, which was in a tiny oasis of posh dwellings surrounded by thousands of council houses, occupied almost exclusively by car workers at the Halewood factory and their families, she had not a word of sympathy to offer me about Mammy. The opposite was true.

She stood in the doorway, hands on hips and dressed in one of the ankle-length skirts she always wore, and glared down at me. 'We shan't miss her,' she hissed. 'If you want to know what I think, it's good riddance to bad rubbish.'

And during the next three weeks she took every opportunity to remind me of her sickening verdict on my mammy.

Her first order to me was to forbid me to call her just Grandma. To me, she was Grandma Seed, and to remind me if I slipped up she kept a special cane that she would wield, with some pleasure, I suspected, across my bare backside.

Her daughter, whom I was instructed to address as Aunt Sheila and never as 'Auntie', was at that time only slightly less frosty. But she mellowed considerably after her mother died, and years later became a kind and caring maiden aunt to me. She was a district nurse and a spinster, who had given up her own chance of marriage to care for her mother, who in return treated her as a slave.

Sheila had once been in love with the famous entertainer George Formby, who had been a close friend of my father when they were fellow borders at St Joseph's College in Dumfries in Scotland. Daddy used to take him home to Halewood for holidays, and that's when the singer began dating my aunt. It might have progressed, but, after her husband died in 1946, Grandma Seed refused to let her daughter leave home and be with George, and the romance fizzled out.

Nothing was simple or casual in Grandma Seed's home. For everything there was a specific place, and it was expected to stay in it, and that included me. I was allowed to sit only on certain chairs and was permitted to watch only one hour's television a day. Grandma Seed sat in a 1930s armchair, very austere and not at all comfortable, to the right of the fireplace. The television was in the corner of the room on the other side of the fireplace, giving her a direct view. Sheila sat directly in front of the fire and my seat was against the wall, which meant I was watching everything at an impossible angle of 30 degrees. And because they thought themselves so grand, I was forced to 'dress properly' in shirt and tie all the time, even to watch television. Radio was confined to the dining room and only during meals.

Grandma Seed was a snob and never tired of telling me that in marrying my mother her son had strayed way beneath his own class. As for me, I had no class at all, she said.

'You are dirt,' she told me on more than one occasion. 'It's a great pity we can't just wash you away.'

She had a dog, a lazy and bad-tempered Yorkshire terrier which would frequently pass wind with a loud explosion of foul-smelling gases. Grandma Seed would smile her evil smile and say, 'Please, Michael, can't you control yourself?' and chuckle to herself.

It wasn't very funny the first time she said it, but it always amused her and she never tired of her little joke.

In truth, the dog was responsible for most of the smells in that house. It always sat too close to the fire and its awful body smell filled the whole place.

I swear, though, that that dog received better treatment than me. He slept in a warm blanket-lined basket in the kitchen. I was banished to the only upstairs room in the bungalow, an attic bedroom which had no heating. A throwback to the Victorian era, it was dark, dank and gloomy, with huge horrible furniture and a big lumpy bed. Even the bedclothes were damp and I think my grandmother deliberately didn't air them before she put them on my bed. They were always clammy and stuck to my body when I first climbed in.

During those three weeks, I spent most of my time grieving and alone, banished to my room, which was one of Grandma Seed's favourite punishments. The rest of the bungalow could be deliciously warm but my room was always cold. She would say in her coldest voice, 'Get out of my sight, you stupid boy,' and point towards the ceiling. That was my signal to go directly to my room.

Even my father disliked being around his mother, and just 15 minutes after dropping me off he had made his excuses and was away. Clearly, he much preferred my kind and gentle Nanny Ramsden to his own mother.

Like the witch in Hansel and Gretel, I don't think Grandma Seed liked children at all, and she hated me, I believed, because I was a constant reminder of the mistake Daddy had made in marrying my mother. She frequently told me she was appalled that the Seed name would be carried on by such a wretched and backward boy as me.

One of her most calculated pieces of nastiness occurred towards the end of my first week there, though

I didn't realise just how spiteful it was until I was much older. 'Well,' she announced at breakfast, which we took, like all our other meals, in the dining room, 'we're finally shot of your mother. Her funeral was yesterday.'

When I asked her what she meant, she smiled her wicked, sneering smile and told me my mother had been burned in a furnace and her remains reduced to ash and shovelled into a hole in the ground in Bolton Cemetery. 'Though she committed a mortal sin by killing herself and should not have been buried with other decent Christians, as there is no chance of her going to heaven,' she added.

'But Nanny said she was already in heaven and was an angel who would watch over me,' I told her.

At this, she laughed and told me, 'That's typical Salvation Army mumbo-jumbo. You're a Catholic boy and shouldn't believe such nonsense.'

When I started to cry, her smile became even wider. She seemed to be gloating over my misery.

Neither she nor my aunt had considered it worthwhile to tell me in advance about Mammy's funeral. Not that I really knew what a funeral was at that age. But it did seem that it hadn't occurred to anyone that I might have wanted to be there to say a proper last goodbye to her. As it turned out, Grandma Seed and her daughter were invited but declined to go. What hurt me later on was that they hadn't even bothered to consult me.

The remainder of my stay with Grandma Seed was a

running battle of wills, but one that I hadn't the slightest chance of winning. A few skirmishes, yes, but not the big battle.

Time and time again, if I hadn't been ordered to my bedroom I was made to stand in a corner or, the ultimate punishment, made to bend over the arm of a large stuffed chair and whacked across my bottom with a cane. And, unlike the priest at my school in Bolton, Grandma Seed made me drop my trousers and pants and laid it on across my bare buttocks.

When Daddy came to Halewood to collect me at the end of my stay, three things were very plain. I hated being there, Grandma Seed hated having me there and Nanny Ramsden very much wanted me to return to Bolton.

Predictably, Grandma Seed's last words were neither caring nor loving. 'I'm glad to see the back of him,' she told Daddy. 'This stupid little boy is no grandchild of mine and that's for sure. Good riddance.'

Just as with Mammy, she was happy to see me gone. But not half as happy as I was to be leaving her. It would have been for ever if I could have had my way, though by now I should have understood that nothing ever happened my way.

The 23-mile drive from Halewood to Bolton took place in total silence as usual. Obviously, Daddy had nothing to say to me and I could think of nothing I wanted to say to him. I was just longing to see Nanny again; to be able to talk to somebody about Mammy without them constantly doing her down.

Even the certain knowledge that I would again be exposed to regular beatings from Daddy and Granddad, and to Daddy's upsetting nocturnal demands, couldn't dampen my joy at escaping the clutches of the Wicked Witch. All that mattered was that I would be with Nanny again – the only person in the whole world who could offer me love.

Chapter Eighteen

Between them, Nanny and my headmaster saved both my life and my sanity through the next few harrowing years of my youth.

Mr Bleasdale became like a second father to me, and a kinder, more helpful and supportive father than the one that fate had already handed me. He was tall and thin and had a small moustache and a permanent hangdog expression, and ages before smoking was considered a social disease he chain-smoked long thin cigars.

Had it been left to the teachers, I might, in time, have struggled through this bad period. They were all kind and gentle with me, and Mr Bleasdale told me I should come to school only when I wanted to. It was the other children who were the problem. They continued to be as ruthless and pitiless as only children can be. They knew every gruesome detail of my mother's suicide, which had been splashed across not just the Bolton Evening News but the Sunday national newspapers too.

I was mocked, taunted and verbally abused almost from the moment I set out on my journey to school in the morning to when I trudged my unhappy way home in the afternoon.

If I did go to school, I almost always refused to go into the playground at break times or at midday. If I did venture outside, this was the signal for the start of a barrage of insults and vicious questions. Some of the children would even mime being a grotesquely broken corpse. I was spat at and kicked as all the while they vied with one another to see who could regale me with the goriest details of my mother's death. They claimed my mother was mad and a witch.

'Your mother's scattered in bits,' they would yell. 'We've seen her blood splattered on the front of trains.'

'Why don't you kill yourself too?' they would chant, and when I didn't answer they would push and punch me.

It became so bad that I couldn't leave the house outside of school hours without being beaten and bullied.

I wanted to scream back that I would love to kill myself. It was what I wanted more than anything else. But each time I came close to doing it something held me back. I don't know if it was just cowardice or whether I didn't want to leave Nanny for the unknown. But I couldn't go through with it.

I would stand on the railway bridge from which Mammy had jumped and wait for the trains to see if there really was blood on the front of any of them, imagining her beautiful body being dismembered by the wheels.

On several occasions, I climbed on to the top of the guard wall and looked down, waiting for a train to come so that I could hurl myself down in front of it.

I felt abandoned, forsaken. There was no future for me. I simply wanted to die. But I couldn't. Each time I would promise myself that I was going to jump and as the train approached I would close my eyes and tell myself, 'Now.' But each time I couldn't go through with it, and that made me feel that somehow I was letting Mammy down and I hated myself for it.

I couldn't talk to anyone about my feelings and became more and more withdrawn, avoiding even the few friends I had. I would wait until after the time to go to school and then go to the big park near by and spend the whole day there alone, wandering and sitting and hurting. I wondered if this was the way Mammy had felt, and whether she had come to the park all those times when she had disappeared from the house for the whole day.

After Mammy's death, my father spent little time at the house, and for this I was very grateful, because our mutual tragedy had not altered his attitude towards me in the slightest. He still beat me, sometime savagely, and forced me, with escalating threats and occasional physical 'persuasion', to indulge him in his vile night-time activities.

As before, my cries of pain in the night never brought Granddad or Nanny to my rescue, and on only one further occasion were the beatings my father gave me ever mentioned between the two men. It happened at breakfast, when I was sporting a black eye after a particularly nasty bedroom session the previous night.

To my regret and disappointment, this time Granddad did not punch Daddy on the jaw and knock him on his backside. But he did stand over him at the breakfast table and punch him quite hard, and repeatedly, on the shoulder while he told him to stop hitting me.

'It's your last warning, Joe Seed,' he stormed. 'If you want to be master in the house, then you'd better get your own bloody house, because you won't do it in mine. This is the last time I'm going to tell you. If it happens again, you'll be out of here, and this time there'll be no sneaking back in.'

Daddy's only response was to nod meekly. He may have been an inch or so taller than Granddad but, like most bullies, he was a coward when someone called his bluff.

It didn't change anything, of course, but what none of us knew at the time was that I would only have to put up with the two of them for another month.

In fact, Granddad's attacks on me had stopped

altogether. It may be that Mammy's suicide had affected him more than he cared to openly admit, or that age and illness were finally telling on him, but we rarely heard his voice raised in anger any more and he now spent most of his waking hours in his favourite chair in the living room. Neither watching television nor listening to the radio, he would just sit there dozing or perhaps daydreaming.

It meant one less trial for me at home, but meanwhile pressures on me outside the home were fast becoming unmanageable. I recognise now that at this point in my life I had become mentally ill.

Mr Bleasdale must have spotted the danger signs because he called in the Bolton Social Services and they appointed a special inspector to look after me. His name was Mr Maurice Ffelan, a bearded man in his early twenties who had recently graduated from university. He was unlike anyone I had ever met before.

He took me on days out, which we spent in the park or in the countryside, chatting about anything and everything. Part of his wisdom was that he never talked to me directly about my problems, but simply spent as much time as possible with me, listening to everything I had to say. He was the first person to whom I was able to open up and discuss my real feelings, though some things were still taboo, like the beatings I received at home and the things Daddy made me do to him in bed.

Mr Ffelan must have realised the amount of damage that had been done to me already, because he arranged for me to see a psychiatrist. Unfortunately, I took an instant dislike to her. She had enormous glasses, like Dame Edna Everage, and was more witchlike than my grandmother in Halewood and even more frightening.

Nanny had to accompany me to these sessions at a special clinic in Bolton and I think she found them just as strange as I did. I would sit in front of the psychiatrist and do little games with blocks and circles and draw shapes. She tried to get me to answer her questions but I refused to say anything. I wasn't communicative.

I had blocked out everything and was totally withdrawn. Even if I could have brought myself to talk to the psychiatrist, how could I have told her about my intimate thoughts in front of Nanny, who sat in on all our meetings?

At every weekly session, I hated the blocks and the games I was asked to play and in the end I wouldn't do anything at all. As an eight-year-old, I don't think there was any way the woman could have counselled me on my loss or my problems, even if she had fully understood what they were.

I had become utterly withdrawn. I was off the Richter scale. But when I was with Mr Ffelan it was different. Then there were just the two of us and he never tried to draw me out or got me to play stupid games. He became a very good friend.

But in the end I simply could not stay at that school, and everyone knew it. I needed a new environment, they said, where I wasn't known and nobody would know about my mother's suicide. What I needed was to switch to a school away from Bolton, I was told, but I did need to go on attending school in order to get a proper education.

After the social workers talked with Daddy, it was decided that this was the right thing to do. I would go back to Halewood and live permanently with the Wicked Witch. But none of those charged with my care realised how much I loathed Grandma Seed. As with everything else in my life, I had always refused to talk about my feelings towards her, so nobody knew the extent of the horror they were sending me back to.

But even I could never have guessed how truly horrible my life was about to become.

Chapter Nineteen

The Scouse accent is unique, and in their devotion to all things Liverpudlian the majority of that city's people are true zealots, unshakeably proud of the way they talk. And that boded ill for me.

It is hard to imagine that I could have been judged more alien by my new fellow pupils if I had gone out of my way to provoke them. I spoke with a Manchester accent while they, without exception, spoke pure Scouse. I was a stranger arriving at a new school, the Catholic primary school of St Andrew the Apostle, at age eight when the others had all started there aged five and knew one another.

I lived in a privately owned bungalow in an exclusive enclave with a snobbish well-off grandmother, while they all came from working-class, mostly hard-up families who lived on council estates.

On top of that, I was an illiterate dunce suffering from severe withdrawal problems and had to make weekly visits to the council psychiatrist. I was as different from them as it was possible to be. In short, I was the perfect victim.

It was a nightmarish scenario and was never destined to have a happy ending. From day one, I faced physical and verbal attacks; the second were not as gross as in Bolton, because these children had not heard about my mother's suicide, but their jibes hurt me all the same, just as their blows did.

Perversely, I could only identify with those same council-house kids who despised me. The children who lived in our road, Mansell Drive, were all from snobbish homes like mine and considered themselves a cut above the council hordes who lived on their doorstep. But I too was considered an outsider and they looked down their noses at me. It was a ridiculous situation. They considered me too common and the kids at my school thought I was too posh.

The residents of our tiny cul-de-sac lived in almost siege-like conditions. At the end was an enormous wall that divided us from the council estates beyond, and behind every house was a massive fence topped with barbed wire, to keep the council tenants at bay. To the Wicked Witch and her neighbours, what lay on the other side of those physical barriers was as alien to them as the far side of the moon.

Sometimes I managed to sneak away into the forbidden area beyond the wall and play with some of the younger children. I was occasionally invited into their homes by the other kids' parents and made very welcome, and would be given things to eat like mushy peas and chips, which I loved. But, on those very rare occasions when I risked taking one of my few friends home with me, my grandmother was incredibly rude to them and ordered the 'council scum' out of her house.

None of this helped my reputation at St Andrew the Apostle, where I continued to ignore classwork and learned precisely nothing. I supposed that the headmaster and teachers in Halewood had been briefed by social services and my headmaster in Bolton, because I was never punished for mentally absenting myself from classes.

Often I went for days without speaking. The teachers knew never to ask me questions and I learned not to respond to verbal abuse from the children; while at home one of Grandma Seed's favourite punishments was to subject me to the 'silent treatment'. I would be made to stand in a corner for hours on end and was forbidden to speak, and at weekends I would often be confined to my awful attic room for the whole day, banned from having the light on, even though in the winter it was dark by four in the afternoon and it became very scary and lonely up there alone.

It was a form of psychological warfare and Grandma Seed had the power to do anything she wanted.

Sometimes her vindictiveness made me almost hate my dead mother for opting out and leaving me a slave to someone else's whims.

In the whole time I stayed with her, the Wicked Witch never once used the word 'please' when she told me to do something or 'thank you' after I performed some chore she had set me. Her comments were nearly all demeaning: 'stupid little boy', 'naughty boy', 'hateful child', or brief orders such as 'Shut up', 'Be quiet' or, the most frequent, 'Silence, boy'.

Mealtimes were a constant battle of wills. There was none of the delicious food that Nanny gave me, like egg and chips or shepherd's pie. I recognise now that the Seeds followed a far healthier diet, with lots of fresh vegetables and fish, but it wasn't food I was used to and I didn't like it.

Grandma Seed would torture me if I didn't eat everything she put on my plate. She would pinch my arms and any other exposed parts of my body and pull little clumps of hair from my temples, where it hurt the most. Sometimes she and my aunt would try to force-feed me, just as Daddy had done, and I wondered if this was something that had happened to him when he was a boy.

The first time was when we were eating fish and spinach and leeks. To me all three were revolting. They had finished theirs but I hadn't eaten a single mouthful when Grandma Seed set to. She brought a clothes peg from the kitchen and, while Aunt Sheila held my arms to my sides, she fastened it on my nose and squeezed my cheeks with the fingers and thumb of one hand, forcing my mouth to open. Then, with the other hand, she tried to spoon a mixture of the stuff on my plate into my mouth.

I struggled and kicked out, but my chair was well forward, pressing my tummy against the edge of the table, and my flailing legs were trapped underneath the table, where I couldn't hurt my attackers.

But in the end nature took its course and I suddenly vomited, not only all over the plate and tablecloth but also on to Grandma Seed's dress. She screamed and leaped backwards and then started to whack me on the sides of my head with her open palms.

My ears rang from the pummelling, and then I threw up again, this time over myself and the carpet.

Aunt Sheila finally released me and I pulled the clothes peg from my nose and covered my head with my arms. But this time I refused to cry. I stifled the sobs in my throat. I was not, I swore to myself, going to give them the satisfaction of reducing me to tears.

I don't know how long I sat there, with my eyes tight shut and my arms wrapped around my head, but when I looked again Grandma Seed was standing there with a bucket and a cloth and a large spoon.

'I've a good mind to make you lick it all up, you filthy little animal,' she hissed. 'But you can clean your own mess up with these,' she added, handing me the spoon and cloth.

I had to spoon up as much of my vomit and spilled food as I could and wipe up the rest with the cloth, then pour the whole lot down the toilet and wash out the bucket and cloth in the kitchen.

Then she ordered me to wash myself and go to bed. There was no question of my having anything to eat. It meant lying there, in my damp sheets, with a rumbling tummy, until sleep rescued me, but I had the satisfaction of knowing that Grandma Seed hadn't won.

They hadn't made me eat. And they hadn't made me cry. Tiny victories perhaps, but I desperately needed some victories, however tiny.

They tried the same tactic again a week later, and with the same result, so after that they never tried to force-feed me again.

Grandma Seed simply changed her approach, and made me sit in front of my untouched food until bedtime. Often it meant going to bed without any dinner, but it was no worse than it had been in Manchester, and I was far too stubborn to seek a compromise. I was losing at everything else in life, so I felt I had to win this battle with Grandma Seed, no matter what the cost.

Even Aunt Sheila would sometimes lose her temper with her mother. It would have been difficult for an outsider to spot, but I learned to recognise the signs. When she was angry, her mouth would go very tight and round and she would call her 'Florence'. A small thing, but it was like a warning slap in the face for Grandma

Seed, who would pull in her witch's claws and go easy with my aunt until she reverted to calling her 'Mum'.

During the rest of that year, Daddy came to visit only three times, though he could never have been more than about 25 miles away. Not seeing him didn't matter to me any more. To satisfy the curiosity of the few kids I did talk to in Halewood, I had reinvented my mother and father. They were a beautiful couple who lived in an exotic location abroad, where they pursued glamorous jobs. I wished with all my heart that Daddy really did live abroad and never came to see me, for in his case absence did not make the heart any fonder, and he gave me a sound thrashing during each of his visits.

The odd thing is that he carried out each of these attacks in front of his mother, almost as though he was performing them for her benefit. These occasions, when he beat me and reduced me to tears in her presence, were some of the rare occasions when I saw Grandma Seed smile. I'm convinced she derived pleasure from watching Daddy pummel me with his fists. What surprised me was that she didn't actually clap her hands in approval.

I doubt, though, that she would have liked what her 'dearest son' later made me do to him in bed, in the privacy of my attic bedroom, before the bruises had properly darkened.

The last time I saw Daddy was on Christmas Day in 1966, the most miserable Christmas in my life, though it hadn't started out that way. Carol singers had come to our front door on Christmas Eve and sung 'We Wish You A Merry Christmas' and 'Oh Little Town Of Bethlehem', and Aunt Sheila had taken them mince pies and allowed me to put some coins in their collecting box. For a short time, I let myself dream that this was going to be a merry Christmas for me.

But later, when I was asleep, Daddy came to my room and got into bed with me and forced me, with whispered threats and a hand clutching my throat so tight I could scarcely breathe, to perform the usual revolting service for him.

It was our first meeting in nearly two months and he hadn't even said hello.

Christmas Day fell on a Sunday that year and the Wicked Witch insisted that we all go, as was her preference, to Bishop Eton Monastery for Mass, which oddly, for me, turned out to be the brightest part of the day. The monastery wasn't our nearest place of worship but had a prestigious reputation, and was in Woolton, one of the richest and most snobbish suburbs of Liverpool.

Lunch, with none of the crackers and paper hats which the Ramsdens so much enjoyed at Christmas, took place, like all our meals in Grandma Seed's house, in the dining room, and in silence until almost at the end, when she insisted I eat all my greens before I could have any pudding. She had deliberately and maliciously piled my plate with Brussels sprouts and broccoli, even though she knew I didn't like them. I had forced down a few mouthfuls but she ordered me to finish every scrap on my plate.

Help came from an unexpected quarter. 'It is Christmas, Mum. Perhaps just this once he can be allowed to leave it,' said Aunt Sheila.

'Rubbish,' snapped her mother. 'There are millions of starving children around the world who would do anything for the chance to eat what he's got. If he won't eat it, then no pudding and no presents.'

Having no pudding was not a hardship, as I only really liked the sherry butter and the cream, but no presents? I hadn't even known that presents were an option, as they hadn't been mentioned before. But even that temptation wasn't enough to induce me to eat that pile of soggy green stuff on my plate.

'No,' I said.

'Did it speak?' Grandma Seed demanded to know of the others. 'Did that revolting piece of filth actually dare to speak?' She looked hopefully towards Daddy, whose eyes had narrowed.

'Stop being such an ungrateful little toad and do what your grandma tells you, or I can promise you'll regret it.'

Now we were in well-trodden territory and I shivered in frightened anticipation of the pain about to be visited on me.

Grandma Seed's eyes glittered. She knew what was coming as well, I could tell, and seemed to be eagerly looking forward to my getting another beating.

But even the thought of spoiling her fun wasn't enough

to make me eat the greens. I just accepted my fate, as I always did. I was too small and weak to do anything else.

'I can't,' I said, knowing that with those words I was done for.

Grandma didn't have long to wait for her entertainment. Daddy pushed back his chair and strode out of the room, before returning moments later swinging the dog's lead, a leather and metal-chain affair, which he had doubled over.

He came straight around the table and hauled me from my seat by the hair, pushed me to the floor on my knees and began to flog me on the back and bottom with the lead.

I began to scream and Grandma Seed began to giggle. Even through my pain, I tried to work out what she must be finding so funny about the situation.

'We wish you a merry Christmas.' Fat chance.

After my beating, I was kicked upstairs, in the dark and the damp, for the rest of Christmas Day, with nothing more to eat or drink.

Until I fell asleep, I kept repeating the words of that Christmas carol in my head. 'We wish you a merry Christmas.'

I hoped Nanny Ramsden was wishing me a merry Christmas, but I could think of few other people on earth who would be wishing the same. Certainly not the Wicked Witch and her awful offspring downstairs.

I don't think I had been asleep for long when Daddy shook me roughly awake.

'Get on with it,' is all he said, and I knew, even though only half-awake, what he wanted, but I just didn't have the will to try to fight it. I just kept repeating over and over again in my mind, 'We wish you a merry Christmas,' as I did what was necessary.

Then I rolled over and went to sleep.

In the morning, when I awoke, Daddy had already gone. I didn't know it then, but he was, in fact, gone from my life for good. Within a month, he became ill and was taken to hospital, where they diagnosed a brain tumour.

My last memories of him will always be of a sadistic beating and being used as his sex slave. His final revolting climax is the only goodbye I will remember.

Christmas would never be quite the same again.

What a ghastly year, and in my sorry isolation I never knew that the England soccer team had won the World Cup.

And I never did get my presents.

Chapter Twenty

My evil grandmother told me that my father's illness had caused his face to become very deformed and that he now resembled a character in the worst kind of horror movie. It's not difficult to imagine the appalling effect that crudely worded statement had on an impressionable and imaginative nine-year-old.

The most noticeable result was a series of terrible nightmares in which I usually pictured Daddy in bed, next to me, forcing me to do things to him, while he snarled threats through rotting teeth in a gash of a mouth set in a terrifyingly distorted face.

I would wake up in the middle of the night screaming with horror and drenched in sweat, but nobody ever came to comfort me, or even ask what was the matter, and if I did try to explain my nightmares to Grandma Seed she would grin in that gloating way she had and, far from easing my fears, give me even more lurid details of Daddy's deformities.

Had I been able to see him, just once, I am sure the reality would not have been anywhere near as bad as my imagination painted it, but I was forbidden to go with Grandma Seed and Aunt Sheila to the hospital. It would be too frightening and distressing, they said, and Grandma would grin her evil grin again. I'm convinced it was because she preferred to torture me with her own deliberately twisted description of my father's disfigurement. Her determination to break my spirit was relentless.

I'll never know for certain what might have happened had I gone on living with her, but I believe that, had I been left in her care for much longer, I would have found a way of escaping – and that would probably have been achieved by killing myself.

She was one of the only truly evil people I believe I have ever encountered in my life, and I have no doubt that she really hated me as much as she made me hate her. Despite all this, my heart and faith have since led me to forgive her. Though I admit it wasn't easy.

But once again my lovely Nanny Ramsden came to my rescue and, in typical story-book ending, rescued me from the Wicked Witch in the nick of time.

With my father dying in hospital and officially registered as incapable, Nanny managed to have herself appointed my legal guardian, and her first act with this new authority was to summon me back to live with her in Bolton.

What joy!

Even the unpleasant prospect of a return to St Osmund's and further confrontation with my playground tormentors appeared a far more attractive proposition than life with Grandma Seed and her unremitting cruelty. She made no attempt to oppose the order, and it was unquestionably evident that my departure was just as welcome to her as it was to me.

'I'm glad to be rid of you,' she hissed, after breaking the news to me that I would soon be leaving. 'You were not wanted when you came here and you're not wanted now. I should never have given you house room. You should have been taken into care, where you belong. Not in a decent home with decent people. You're a nasty, horrid little boy and no good will ever come of you. Mark my words, you'll come to a bad end, and it's what you deserve. Good riddance to you is what I say. Good riddance.'

I know I could have let it be and left her house without any further punishment, but I also knew inside that something had to be said on behalf of Mammy and myself. I had to make a last stand against Grandma Seed and I was prepared to have my ears boxed as the price of saying my piece – and that's exactly what happened. But it was worth it, just to tell her to her face, 'Mammy was right about you. You are a witch,' I yelled. 'The Wicked Witch of the West.'

It was Aunt Sheila who drove me back to Bolton and all the way home I hugged myself with satisfaction for having had the courage to say what I felt. It was worth a hundred slaps around the face for the rare and exquisite pleasure of seeing the shock on her face when I unmasked her as the witch she really was.

Mammy would have loved it too.

On this occasion Aunt Sheila actually entered Nanny's house to hand me over, and, though she wasn't friendly, she was at least courteous, and Nanny thanked her, just as politely, for bringing me home.

It was a wonderful reunion. Nanny hugged me and kissed me and made a tremendous fuss, and I revelled in it all. It had been more than a year since I was taken from her to live with Grandma Seed, and she told me I had a year of hugs owing to me.

Even Granddad managed a smile and a welcome, though I noticed straight away that there had been big changes in him. Somehow he looked smaller sitting in his chair and his eyes didn't look as sharp. Even his voice seemed frailer and he no longer exuded the aggression and intimidation of before. At that moment I suddenly realised that I wasn't frightened of him any more.

All at once, the future started to look quite rosy. Daddy was safely tucked away in hospital and unlikely to return, the Wicked Witch was out of my life for ever and I was to have my own warm, big bedroom with a big bed which nobody but I would ever sleep in. That's when I started daring to believe that everything was going to be all right.

I should have known better, of course. Within days, these fragile feelings of happiness were smashed to smithereens.

Chapter Twenty-One

To give him his due, Mr Bleasdale did do his best to protect me. During morning assembly, on my first day back at St Osmund's, he read the riot act to the other children. He assured them that anyone caught bullying me would be savagely punished, promising six of the best with his cane to anyone who defied his order.

The effect was certainly not what he had been anticipating. It was as though he had announced open season on Michael Seed. Some of them couldn't even wait until playtime to have a go at me. During our first lesson of the day, they passed me disgusting drawings and whispered vile comments about my mother. And at playtime many took the open risk of defying Mr

Bleasdale, teasing and poking me, even though a teacher was there noting their names for later caning.

Their behaviour was barbaric. Not content with pinching and punching, some of them would even stick hat pins into my arms, though it was the spitting I disliked the most. Sometimes my face would run with their revolting saliva. It would get in my eyes and ears and hair. I just hated it.

After school, the bullying intensified. That's where the real nastiness occurred.

My worst tormentors were a wicked and vicious clique of ten-year-old girls who had for some reason picked on me as their primary victim. They were the ringleaders, who, through their own example of verbal and physical assaults, or by maliciously egging the pack on, would provoke their brothers and other boys to chase me along the pavement, hurling bricks and stones, along with their expletives, as I ran for home.

These screeching bullies made my life an absolute hell, and had it not been for my self-appointed band of bodyguards I would have been regularly kicked and beaten to a pulp. These were a handful of boys who lived close to my grandmother's house and had befriended me when I first arrived in Bolton at the age of seven. Only one of them was as big, or slightly bigger, than me, while the others, including Peter, my favourite, were much smaller.

Looking back on it, this Praetorian guard they so proudly formed to look after me was, in reality, a shrimps' squad. But it was never more true to say that what they lacked in size they more than made up for in courage, and they became my guardian angels. They took many of the punches and missiles aimed at me and themselves became the victims of the school bullies when they were caught alone.

I will be eternally grateful to those brave young protectors of mine. They prevented, or at least deflected, some of the vilest abuse and physical attacks from the intended victim, and asked for nothing but my friendship in return. On occasion, they literally saved my life.

One of the most dramatic incidents occurred in early winter, and followed shortly after another most significant happening in Raikes Road in November.

Granddad Ramsden had grown progressively weaker during the autumn and had developed a constant hacking cough. It was painful just to have to listen to him. After each bout of coughing, he would sit in his chair, shaking all over from the effort of coping with his agony.

In mid-November, he became so ill that Nanny could no longer nurse him at home and an ambulance came to collect him and take him to the hospital in Bolton.

My last glimpse of him was of his pinched grey face, just visible over the edge of a dark blanket as they lifted him into the ambulance.

A few days later, I was delivered safely home by my protectors to find Nanny waiting by the front gate in tears. Clutching me to her, she told me that Granddad had died that afternoon. I suppose I should have cried, but I couldn't. I felt no sense of loss at all. Indeed, my first inward reaction had been: 'Well, that's one less.' For this was a man who had frequently punched me black and blue for no reason, and did nothing to protect his own daughter being beaten up and driven to suicide while living in his house.

I felt sad for Nanny. But that was all.

Suddenly, we had become a two-person family, and it was I, Nanny now declared, who had to be the man of that family. I didn't feel very manly, spending most of my time outside of classroom and home, it seemed, running away from a growing number of children whose dearest wish, they said repeatedly, was to see me dead.

Soon after Granddad's funeral, which Nanny chose not to let me attend, my persecutors' dearest wish was nearly granted.

It happened on a Saturday morning. I was playing with two of my friends in No Man's Land. There were always dead mice and rats near the tip there and we would play a morbid game called Funerals, which I now understood only too well, in which we made coffins out of scrap cardboard and string and wire and buried the vermin in little graves marked with wooden crosses.

Suddenly, we found ourselves under attack from a screaming group of boys and girls from school. They raced down on us, hurling sticks and stones and pieces of metal, missiles that were scattered around in plenty in No Man's Land.

We immediately abandoned the mouse burial we were performing and took off fast. There were only three of us and about a dozen of them, so there was no question of staying to fight. We would have been slaughtered.

As we ran, I heard Peter yell, 'Look out,' but I was too scared to stop and find out what the problem was. I realised soon enough, as my feet started to slide from under me. The warning Peter had been shouting was that we were about to run out on to the iced-over pond. By that time I was out in the centre of the pond, whose water beneath the ice I knew was filled with filth and oil. Having tested it earlier on, I also knew that the ice was not very thick.

Peter and my other friend had separated and run around the edges of the pond but our pursuers, seeing me stopped in the middle, gathered by the edge, 20 or 30 feet away, and began throwing large stones and pieces of brick. I was aware instantly what they were trying to do – smash the ice and cause me to plunge into the horrible mixture underneath.

I started to edge towards the far bank, but they quickly realised what I was doing and spread out around the pond, trapping me. My friends had retreated to a hillock 50 yards away, from where they could do little but watch.

Once the gang knew they had me surrounded, their cries, like those of the circling Indians in the Saturday-morning films, became louder and their tactics bolder.

They soon realised that the ice around the edges of the pond was thicker and stronger than it was at its centre, and some of them, braver than the others, took a few paces towards me before launching their missiles at me.

Under such a bombardment, it was only a matter of time before the inevitable happened and the ice gave way.

When it did happen, it was both dramatic and fast. A large slab of concrete, hurled by one of the bigger boys, landed only a foot or so away from me. There was a sudden loud report and jagged cracks raced out across the ice in every direction. At the spot where the missile had landed, a large slab of ice tilted and the concrete slid beneath the surface. At almost the same moment, the ice on which I was standing disappeared from beneath my feet and I plunged into the freezing black liquid below.

As my head went under, I could hear my attackers' whoops of triumph, mixed with laughter from some of the girls.

When I surfaced I was in a hole about six feet square, and out of my depth. I grabbed hold of the edge of the ice and tried to pull myself out but my hands kept skidding off and sending me back under.

I was screaming with fear by now. 'Please help me.'

But not one of my tormentors made a move to assist me, even though they must have understood by this time that I was in real danger of drowning.

Instead, with barely a backward glance, and still a good deal of laughter, they turned their backs on the pond and headed in a group towards Raikes Road.

The cold was worse than I had ever experienced and I could feel my strength running out as I tried again and again to pull myself out of the water and on to the ice. But it was impossible.

Then I heard Peter's voice. He had found a long broken branch and was crawling out on to the ice, pushing it in front of him.

'Grab on, Michael, and I'll pull you out,' he yelled.

I went under again, but this time, when I surfaced, I found the ends of the branch awaiting my fingers instead of bare ice. I clung on and shouted, 'I've got it.'

Peter began crawling backwards and I heard the voice of our other friend say, 'I've got the end too, Michael. Hang on.'

Then came a strange thought: let go now and it will all be over. No one can ever hurt you again.

The temptation to let go and allow myself to slip beneath the water for a final time was almost overwhelming, but not quite. Something inside refused to let me give in. If I died now, I told myself, those kids would have won. It was one thing for me to kill myself, which I might do at any time, but it was a very different thing for my enemies to kill me.

I clung to that branch with all my remaining strength, and as my rescuers crawled backwards, tugging me with them, gradually, hand over hand, I started to haul myself out of the water.

With the arms of my two brave friends supporting me from either side, we staggered back to Nanny's house and told her simply that I had fallen through the ice while we were playing.

I must have looked a sorry bedraggled figure, but Nanny, as always, had a remedy and an answer. She stripped me and stood me in front of the kitchen fire and rubbed me down with a large white bath towel.

Her answer to why I had nearly drowned?

I had recently, on 13 November, along with all the other kids of my age at school, been confirmed into the Catholic faith, at St Osmund's Church by the local bishop, Thomas Holland, and Nanny, still a strict Salvationist, had not approved.

'No good will come of this,' she had muttered at the time.

Now, as she rubbed me pink and warm with the towel, she chided, 'I told you no good would come of that Catholic nonsense, didn't I? Tomorrow we'll go to the Salvation Army service and make sure the hex is well and truly off you.'

Nanny smiled. My soul and my safety would soon be back in the right hands.

At that moment, as far as my soul was concerned, I couldn't have cared less. Catholics, Salvationists, anybody could have it.

As for my safety, I doubted anyone could really help in that direction. From infancy to adolescence, and especially right then, the thought of ever feeling safe was just a ridiculous dream.

Chapter Twenty-Two

Children contemplating suicide don't think about it one day and not the next. It is a continual death wish, and not necessarily curable. It is always there, matched and intensified by the absolute misery that is one's prime motivation for destroying oneself.

I know, because the foremost thought in my mind for most of my childhood years was to kill myself, and I tried to do it on many occasions.

Always my favourite scenario was to copy my mother's suicide. I spent countless hours standing on the Long Lane railway bridge or down by the track itself, waiting for a train to come so that I could throw myself into its path. Each time I was determined to carry it through, but each time, as the train rushed towards me, promising blessed oblivion, I drew back at the last moment.

It wasn't because I was a coward, because I had faced and conquered pain, and the threat of terrible violence, on countless occasions in the past, and still faced almost daily beatings from the gangs of school bullies. And it wasn't because I thought that it was wrong to use this way of putting myself out of my misery. It was just something inside, more powerful than my determination to die, that held me back at the last moment.

On two occasions I lay on the track with my neck on the rail, waiting for the train which would mercifully end everything. Both times I lay facing the direction from which the train would come and it was only when it was almost on top of me, and the rail under my neck vibrating madly, that I leaped to my feet and out of harm's way.

I still vividly recall how close the trains passed and how the blast of them tugged at my clothes and my body, trying to drag me under their wheels.

In the end, I think it was the thought of the effect my death would have on Nanny that prevented me killing myself. But I shall never be certain. I just know that in that final moment I was unable to take the step which would have meant terminating my life completely. Not that I had anything particularly attractive, apart from Nanny, to hold me in this world.

The only time that I was not at risk from attack was at

home, for even in the classroom I was never completely safe from the nips and punches and foul whispers. My cuts and bruises seemed never-ending and sometimes it was difficult to hide them from Nanny, perhaps after a bad beating or being struck by a large stone.

I tried to pass off my wounds as the results of a boy's normal, everyday rough and tumble, because I didn't want her to constantly worry about me. She was 73 and I was 10, but I already felt a responsibility for her and didn't want to see her hurt.

Sometimes, though, if the bruises were bigger or angrier than usual, she would insist on my seeing the family doctor. Poor Nanny never discovered that Dr John Monks was a far greater danger to his child patients than any ailment for which they might have been seeking treatment.

The doctor was very grand and extremely posh. He looked like Mr Pickwick and sounded like the great actor Donald Sinden, and he lived in a grand old house in the most exclusive suburb of Bolton. His surgery was inside this house, and sometimes his children, who were about my age, would open the front door to patients. They must have been educated privately because I had never heard children speak with such a grand accent.

Dr Monks was a Conservative alderman who became mayor of Bolton in 1970. We were extremely poor but always voted Conservative, because Dr Monks would pick up Nanny in his limousine on election days and drive her to the polling station to vote. During his year as mayor, he had her collected in his chauffer-driven mayoral car.

Everyone acknowledged that Dr Monks's older partner was a far better doctor, but he was a difficult man and had an appalling bedside manner. If he came to visit Nanny, even though he examined her thoroughly and dealt efficiently with her problem, she would be depressed afterwards.

But, when Dr Monks came, he would sit on the end of her bed, chat with her for a while and give her a handful of pills, and his visit was as good as a tonic.

Everybody liked jovial, laughing Dr Monks, though I suspect only a tiny percentage of his adult patients knew of his secret proclivities.

All the boys in the neighbourhood knew about him, and it was a big joke among us. No matter what was wrong with you, even if you had a sore throat or a headache, you had to drop your trousers and have him feel and squeeze your genitals, sometimes for several minutes at a time. On other occasions, he would sit you on his knee and slide his hand up or down your trousers and fondle you.

The slightly older boys found it a bit embarrassing – I did after I turned 14 – but nobody ever reported him. He was such a friendly jovial character that nobody really minded his persistent groping.

None of the other boys saw Dr Monks as a real threat and even though I know now that what he was doing was wrong, and that he was using his position to prey on boys, when compared with other chapters in my life, I find it difficult to think of his actions as being anything other than comedy rather than abuse.

Other 'victims' must have felt the same, because, to my knowledge, the doctor was never questioned.

In that year of 1968, I had more serious things to think about. In January, my father died. I hadn't seen him for 13 months because he had been in hospital for all that time with a brain tumour, and, like my Grandma Seed, Nanny had decided that I shouldn't visit him because his head and face had become so terribly disfigured.

She was driven to see him every fortnight by one of her neighbours, and told me that towards the end he had asked for me. But even then she had still believed that it would be too upsetting for me to see him. Perhaps he wanted to make amends, or to ask for my forgiveness. I will never know.

Nanny broke the news of his death to me as she had done about the death of my grandfather, waiting at the front gate for me to come home from school. It wasn't a real shock, as I hadn't seen him for over a year, but I felt sort of numb inside. My thoughts went instantly to the last time he had been with me – and whatever sorrow I might have felt died in that instant. I did not cry.

This man had treated Mammy and me with a mean and pitiless savagery which was almost inhuman. But, even though a beast, he was still my father, and at the age of ten you don't dwell on the bad times.

He sought an answer to his problems with violence and, as a result, existed in a loveless hell of his own creation. That, and a slow and agonising death, I believe, were his punishment, and I let it go at that.

Somehow it had come down to Nanny and me against the world. A very eccentric household with each of us clinging on to life for the sake of the other.

The second significant occurrence that year was that Mr Bleasdale, my headmaster, decided to teach me to read, and for a part of each day I sat at his desk with him in his study and belatedly learned my ABC.

By the end of that year, even though I still refused to put my newly acquired skill to work in the classroom, I had, at least, mastered the art of reading.

Chapter Twenty-Three

The progress I had made thanks to Mr Bleasdale didn't stop me, when I came to sit the 11-plus examination, from writing my name at the top of the paper and then sitting there for two hours daydreaming. As usual, I made no attempt to read the questions or to write any of the answers, and left all my papers blank. I couldn't write or express myself on paper in any way and I certainly couldn't do arithmetic.

I had refused to conform for so many years that I was beyond change. I didn't want to be a part of other people's worlds. I didn't care about not belonging. Having retreated into my own isolated existence, I found I liked being there. I just couldn't cope with the ordinary world. I had no desire to study, even though I felt incapable and a failure. It was just another dimension to my general misery.

Not surprisingly, I failed my 11-plus, recording the lowest-ever mark achieved in that exam – zero. No less surprisingly, as a result I was sent to the most dreadful school in the area, St Anne's Catholic Secondary Modern.

There was still a great difference in those days between ordinary secondary schools and grammar schools. Peter and my other guardian angels had all passed their exam and gone on to good grammar schools. I was now heading for a new environment, with no protection against the other children and no friends among the teachers.

On my first morning, I set off alone on the walk of a mile and a half to St Anne's. Nanny was too old to accompany me, though she had made sure I was kitted out properly in my new uniform.

I made a poor start by turning up at the wrong school, having failed to notice that I was in a different uniform from every other child in the playground. Most of the children had been called to their new classes before a teacher spotted that I was the odd boy out and pointed me in the right direction for St Anne's.

Being late made no difference to which class I was assigned to. News of my unique exam mark must have preceded me, because I was placed in the bottom class and told to sit at the back.

St Anne's was a horrible school, filled with horrible

children and horrible teachers. It had no redeeming features. Everything was horrible.

Any faint hope I had held on to that I might have gone unrecognised in my new school was crushed within minutes when, installed in my classroom, I found myself facing some of my worst enemies from St Osmund's.

I don't know why I was so surprised to see them there, for my young tormentors had been among the most unruly and underachieving pupils in my primary school. Their chances of passing the 11-plus had been only marginally better than mine, and I had stood no chance at all of passing.

Within a morning, all the other kids in my class, and probably most of the school, knew about my mother and my sessions with the psychiatrist. I was still the mad kid with the mad mother, and an irresistibly inviting target for everybody's spite and cruelty.

My only defence at this stage was to crawl ever deeper into my shell and become even less sociable than before.

But this didn't save me from regular beatings, for bigger boys would start their bullying the moment they saw me, and, if I wasn't with someone big enough or willing enough to protect me, which was rare, I would always end up with at least a bloody nose.

My only respite from this constant torment came during a week-long school visit to Belgium and Germany.

Nanny thought that, after everything I had been through, this would be a wonderful treat – and so it was. The children who went on the trip proved to be from the better-off and better-behaved element in the school and I wasn't bullied once during the whole week we were away.

The contrast with my normal life in Bolton was incredible. I had never been out of Lancashire and Liverpool in my life, apart from summer trips to Douglas, Isle of Man, with Nanny to stay in a boarding house run by her sister, Ethel Marks. Now I was visiting foreign countries and staying in posh hotels, and had travelled through London and across the sea in a huge boat which had our school bus parked below decks.

Our trip through London was mostly a blur, with distant views of Big Ben and St Paul's Cathedral. I had no way of knowing then, or even imagining, that one day I would make this city my home, know the corridors of the Palace of Westminster better than the streets of Bolton, and number prime ministers and royals among my friends.

I would never give up hope or lose my determination to ultimately triumph in this world, but back then I was simply the most insignificant person who happened to be passing through a great city. It was a foreign wonderland to me, and I really was in a state of wonder.

Staying in a hotel was also a new experience for me. For the first time in my life, I was actually being waited on. Never before had I experienced such a magical time.

That week showed me that other people lived lives that were totally different from anything I had ever experienced. I saw how normal people communicated and impressed one another with hardly any effort. For the very first time in my life, I fitted in and was part of a crowd, and yet the feeling was so overwhelming that it made me feel more depressed than ever before.

But I still felt the warmth of the other boarders, the camaraderie of my companions, including my teachers, and it was marvellous. For the first time, I felt I truly belonged, however long that might last.

There were some little pedal cars at the place we stayed at near Knokke in Belgium, and one morning I decided to pedal off alone. I went for what seemed like miles and it was a very comforting feeling, knowing that nobody knew me and that I could carry on pedalling for ever – never going back.

I could drive until I reached the sea and that would be the end of it all. I would go on until the water covered my head. Then I would join Mammy. I felt at peace with the world. Perhaps this would be the time I could go through with it.

But I was never to know what might have been.

One of my teachers missed me and came looking for me. He found me pedalling furiously away from town.

The teachers were able to laugh about it afterwards, but I still wonder what might have happened if I hadn't been found that day.

PART THREE

PART THREE

Chapter Twenty-Four

After the heavenly luxury of an unmolested week abroad, it was dreadful having to return to the everlasting hell of daily strife in Bolton.

The level of bullying was at an all-time high and for the first time in my life I began to seriously doubt that I could go on taking it. My battered spirit, which had sustained me through the worst that my father and grandfather and Grandma Seed had dished out, couldn't take much more of this kind of battering. The beatings alone I might have coped with, but it was a different thing to have to withstand the sheer magnitude of their combined loathing and contempt.

On top of all that, educationally things were hopeless. I still couldn't study and, though I detested my total academic incompetence, I could do nothing to change it. I was sinking and didn't know how to bail out. More than ever, I wanted to die.

Even my relationship with Nanny had reached an all-time low. Most of the time now, I was depressed and frustrated, upset and angry. She was the only one I felt I could let off steam to and, even though I knew I was taking it out on her because she was available, it didn't stop me throwing terrible tantrums. I was horrible and very aggressive towards her and, though I knew it frightened her and made her depressed, I couldn't stop.

As well as finding me a struggle to cope with, Nanny could no longer look after me properly, and this made her even more upset. She thought she was holding me back.

At the same time, my social worker also thought that my having to care for Nanny was inhibiting my normal development. Mr Ffelan said it was unhealthy for me to be with someone who was getting so old. I was almost totally isolated from everyone else and had very few friends.

I didn't even want to go out any more. I just wanted to stay in my room and hide away. I'd had enough.

After almost a year at St Anne's, I had achieved nothing except to make myself the most unpopular and targeted boy in school.

Somehow, said Mr Ffelan, I had to adjust to living with other people. It was impossible for me to carry on in normal education. I needed to be among other boys like myself. A new school, he explained, had been opened in Rochdale called Knowl View, which was a special school for emotionally and behaviourally disturbed children. This experimental school was destined to remain open for under 20 years and, though it was a disastrous fire that brought about its end, it was ultimately considered to have failed.

In the beginning, however, Knowl View seemed the perfect answer for local authorities trying to rid themselves of their worst problem youngsters – of whom I was one – and we were passed on to the school and scratched from the social workers' register.

Unfortunately for me, most of the boys were sent there for being extremely aggressive and out of parental control. In truth, most of them belonged in a detention centre, and I imagine that many of them ended up behind bars. Others had serious mental problems or were retarded and were incapable of fitting into an ordinary school. Nanny and I knew nothing of all this when Mr Ffelan drove us there to view the school and meet the headmaster.

But, for me, there was not really any other option. The physical and verbal abuse I was suffering at St Anne's had long since reached an intolerable level and I believed that, if things went on unchanged, the other children would kill me.

Nanny didn't want me to go but we both recognised that to carry on as we were was no longer either feasible or desirable.

Neither would Knowl View School turn out to be, despite its sparklingly clean and modern facade. No one told me that it was a school for maladjusted children. But, even if they had, I wouldn't have known what it meant.

My departure brought floods of tears from Nanny and stirred up my terror at leaving an environment I was used to. Despite my fears, I was optimistic because I figured that, as I didn't know anyone in Rochdale, I could completely reinvent myself there, and perhaps even make friends.

Which all proves that at 12 I still had a lot to learn about the vagaries of fate.

Chapter Twenty-Five

Knowl View School, I rapidly discovered, was for neither the timid nor the innocent.

We may have been called pupils, but in reality we were more like prison inmates. Officially, we were not allowed to leave the premises without an escort, when we would go out in convoys, like rows of ducks, led by a teacher. This rule was relaxed when we were older.

Set in lush green acres of playing fields and parkland in a genteel suburb some two miles north-west of Rochdale, the school should have been a paradise, but instead proved to be home to a hard core of young career criminals. A later generation of residents would burn down the place, and it never recovered.

We were a nightmare mix of different cultures, colours and religions.

The thugs, mainly skinheads, several of whom had tattoos that were as intimidating as they were explicit, would sneak out of the dormitories at night and head for the town's red-light district. Some were dealing drugs, others made their 'pocket money' thieving and there was a well-organised contingent of rent boys, selling their bodies to kerb-crawling paedophile homosexuals. Some of them were working the streets during the day, as well as at night, and often barely made it back for the evening check by house staff.

Several of them tried to recruit me into their trade, boasting of the rich pickings to be had from what they called the 'old faggots' who bought their services. They talked in terms of hand jobs and blow jobs and bend-overs, which initially sounded like a foreign language to me, and told me it was money for old rope. Five pounds a time was the going rate for a rent boy in Rochdale in 1970.

For a reclusive boy of 12, whose chief companion for years had been a 73-year-old grandmother, it was frightening and confusing to be plunged into this alien world of casual criminals and sex-for-sale teenagers.

I thought these boys were clearly not short of cash, for several of them wore Ben Sherman shirts, which were all the rage among trendy teenagers at that time.

I was twelve and for once was desperate to conform. I was prepared to do almost anything to possess one of the coveted shirts.

But I also knew that my chance of ever being able to

buy one was absolute zero. We were incredibly poor and nanny had only her pension to live on. There was never anything left over for luxuries. She couldn't even afford to add anything to the few shillings a week pocket money I was given at school.

But that didn't stop the longing to have my own trendy shirt. I was so envious, in fact, that I admitted my secret yearning to one of the other boys.

'I wish I had the money to buy a shirt like yours,' I told him.

He thought it a huge joke and laughed out loud.

'None of us bought these shirts,' he told me. 'We nicked them. It's dead easy. No-one ever gets caught. Just make sure there's nobody watching and stuff it under your jacket. It's a piece of cake.'

I could scarcely sit still, waiting for my next weekend at home so I could go on my first shoplifting expedition.

But, even after reassurances from several of my light-fingered school mates, I was still feeling very nervous as I threaded my way through the various clothes racks and counters in the new C&A shop in Bolton's first shopping mall, the Arndale Centre. Finally, I was standing before a rail filled with the beautiful Ben Sherman shirts.

There were several people in the shop, but I looked around carefully and couldn't see anyone watching. I could feel my courage draining away and knew it was now or never, so I snatched a shirt from its hanger and bundled it up and stuffed it into the inside of my jacket.

It was all over in a few seconds, and had been just as easy as my fellow thieves in school had told me.

I was still congratulating myself as I left the shop, and then a young woman grabbed my arm and spun me round.

'Aren't you going to pay for that shirt?' she asked me.

'What shirt?' I stammered, and could feel my face starting to burn through the combined impact of fear and shame.

'The one under your jacket', she told me. 'You'd better come to the office.'

I started sobbing, but her heart was too tough to be melted by a few tears and half an hour later a uniformed police constable arrived and marched me down to a panda car.

'Am I going to jail?' I asked.

He laughed.

'No son, but you'll probably wish you were when your father finds out.'

In the end a thrashing from my father would have been far more preferable than seeing nanny's reaction.

She was so ashamed at having a policeman come to the house. Angry too, and she slapped me hard. But watching her cry with shame was the hardest thing for me to take.

The incident wasn't mentioned again for another twenty years until I confessed my 'criminal past' to a wonderful lady who had become a dear friend, the late Ingrid Brenninkmeyer.

I had been introduced to her by another good friend,

her neighbour Sir Sigmund Sternberg, a world mover in promoting friendship and co-operation between Muslims, Jews and Christians.

Mrs Brenninkmeyer was a member of the extremely generous, but publicity shy, Dutch philanthropic family, who owned C&A until its closure in Britain in 2000.

She was a saintly lady with an impish sense of humour. When I explained my disastrous sortie into shop-lifting, in one of her family's stores, she laughed and said: 'I didn't realise your connection with my family went back quite so far, Michael. What a naughty boy.'

My 'criminal past' remained a standing joke between us until her death a few years ago.

Being caught red-handed earned me a lot of teasing from the boys at school but was soon forgotten as other, more interesting, gossip emerged.

There were fights and beatings and feuds, just like in prison, and I was occasionally a victim of their violence, but I could only be thankful that even the most aggressive among them were usually too busy with their own bizarre affairs to bother with me. The news that Edward Heath had become Prime Minister never made it past the gates of Knowl View, but the current rates for sex and drugs on the local high street were hot topics for discussion.

There were three distinct types in the school: the children who were not aware, called mentally subnormal in those days, the thugs who suffered from serious behavioural problems, and me. Most of the hooligan types had been badly abused mentally, physically or sexually, and many of them had a parent who was either in prison or addicted to drugs or alcohol, or both.

The school gave scarcely any formal lessons apart from metalwork and woodwork. Each boy was more or less allowed to get on with whatever he fancied doing at the time, though there were compulsory monthly visits to the production lines of dozens of factories across the north of England, and it was very clear that the authorities believed this was the only kind of work we could ever aspire to. As a result, they never attempted to academically equip us for anything more challenging. The only important teaching seemed to be to get us to read and write.

With the exception of the headmaster, Mr Turner, who was a dedicated caring man and someone one could always talk to, the teachers seemed to have difficulty in providing intellectual stimulation or inspiration.

One teacher was particularly repulsive. This brutal low-class individual appeared to thrive on being nasty, referring to us all as 'little shits' and verbally abusing the most susceptible boys. Once he had selected his victim, he would concentrate for the whole lesson on reducing him to tears. He was bordering on sadistic, and I don't understand how people of that mentality manage to get into teaching.

Mr Turner and the psychiatrist apart, most of the resident staff acted more like warders than teachers and seemed not to take much account of our feelings. Some were critical to the point of being cruel. The majority made little or no effort to get to know or understand us, though there were a few teachers who clearly cared about the boys and made a big effort to improve our lives.

One teacher used to complain all the time that we smelled. It was true. We were smelly. Youngsters tend to sweat a lot and we were made to wear our underwear, socks and shirts for three days at a time. Trousers were worn for a couple of weeks between washes. I suppose we were used to the smell, but the teachers must have found a whole class of us pretty overpowering. Sometimes I myself would find the smell in the dormitory unbearable and I tried to leave a window open at night, even in the winter.

The dormitories were open-plan with room for a dozen beds and lockers. We had a wall either side of us for privacy and we each faced another boy's bed across the central walkway. The brown linoleum floors were immaculately clean and the predominant smell, apart from ourselves, was of Dettol. But we weren't the 'pigs in shit' that one teacher used to sneeringly label us.

Ironically, one of the most popular teachers, David Higgins, later became the subject of a police investigation into paedophilia and was convicted of indecent assault on several of the pupils at Knowl View. Like Dr Monks, he had vocationally situated himself to have maximum access to the boys he preyed on.

Even though we had to wear the same underwear for three days, we were made to shower every day, which I thought was marvellous. At home, we had been lucky enough to have had a bathroom with a bath. In those days, many homes still didn't. But I had never had a shower before going to Knowl View and I loved it.

If Mr Higgins had had his way, we would have showered twice a day. Other teachers would come to watch us in the open showers and often make very personal remarks about our genitals, but Mr Higgins was the only one who would touch us. His technique was ingenious. He would take us on hikes or potholing, and because we loved these outings he was by far the most popular teacher. Of course, boys of that age adore mud, so Mr Higgins encouraged us to get as dirty as we liked, and when we returned to the school it was only natural that he should suggest we all have a good shower.

And there would be Mr Higgins, then aged about 30, armed with the soap, helping us to reach the parts we couldn't easily reach. He would give a little rub here and a little rub there. It was the perfect cover for a pervert.

There were five showers in a row and he would have us in five at a time. Sometimes he would wash and play with us and, on occasion, he would get boys to masturbate. At the time, I thought that all this was normal; that it was what they did at boarding school. No one ever seemed to object and the rent boys would joke about giving him 'one on the house'.

To begin with, I hadn't understood some of their comments about Mr Higgins, but in this kind of environment few mysteries survived and, courtesy of Mr Higgins's command performances in the shower, I soon learned about that rite of passage through adolescence, masturbation.

It rapidly opened my eyes to what the rent boys were up to, but it also made me see the utterly selfish reasons behind my father's nocturnal demands and threats, and confirmed that my childish instincts had been spot on. What he had forced me to do was both wrong and shameful.

But even this realisation wasn't enough to make me want to discuss my father's predatory sexual practices with my new psychiatrist. My experiences were far too recent and painful to talk about out loud. They were family secrets that were too raw and horrific to reveal to anyone.

The one thing that all 50 or so boys at Knowl View had in common was a weekly individual meeting with the resident psychiatrist. Like me, at these sessions, none of the boys ever honestly discussed his background or problems. People like the psychiatrist couldn't understand that kids don't open up on demand. We made up lies and acted out fantasy family scenarios rather than reveal the truth.

The psychiatrist was a decent well-meaning man and very different from the lady I used to see in Bolton. We did jigsaws and played games instead of messing about with boxes, but I never found our sessions any help. I knew I wasn't mad and I'm sure he believed the same, but we still had to spend our half-hour together each week. It was, after all, a school for maladjusted children and he had a job to do.

Chapter Twenty-Six

During my first year at Knowl View I underwent two fundamental changes. I became a Strict Baptist, and Mr Stanley Thomas stepped into my life. In truth, it was Nanny who changed faiths after being a lifelong Salvationist, and I just followed suit.

The one weekend a month when I was allowed home became the highlight of my existence. I found I missed Nanny far more than I ever dreamed I would, and I concentrated hard on enjoying every moment we had together.

For these weekend visits, the boys – those who had homes to go to, or were wanted there – had to be driven by a uniformed chauffeur and accompanied by a social worker. I suppose they wanted to make sure we ended up in the right place and were not getting up to mischief. The return journey was different. We were left to make our own way back to school, by bus, train or any other available means.

It was during one of my weekends at home that Nanny announced that she was no longer a Salvationist but had become a Strict Baptist. She was converted by a former fellow Salvationist, Pastor Harold Watson, who had become a travelling evangelist, almost as well known in his day as Billy Graham. When he came to preach in Bolton, Harold contacted my grandmother and that was enough to convince her that we too should become Baptists.

I wasn't afraid of Harold, because he was a family friend, but I found the preachers in the local Baptist church really frightening. They were extreme, even by normal Baptist standards. Sermons lasted at least an hour and were full of fire and brimstone and dire warnings that if one wasn't saved one would spend eternity in the fiery pit of hell. Everyone in that church that day had to be saved.

The problem for me was that not only was I not saved, but I didn't even know what 'saved' meant. I convinced myself that I was going to hell and, as I was still determined to kill myself at some stage, I accepted that would be when I would make the leap into the fiery pit.

I'd already given up on the concept of God. If they had been through the kind of disasters I had encountered in my life, it was quite normal, I thought, for someone to give up on God. But that didn't mean giving up on religion. Not with a Nanny like mine. We would go to Baptist evangelical rallies on Saturdays and church and protests on Sundays. To say she was fervent would be a drastic understatement.

Nanny had a wonderful neighbour, Dorothy Kay, who would drive us to the rallies. She would pray while she was at the wheel, which involved closing her eyes. We were both terrified of her driving and Nanny would frequently remind her, 'It is better to live a little longer in this world than to be too soon in the next.'

Strict Baptists were not what I would call charismatic. The preachers were very emotional, but not the congregation. Our clergy were called pastors and didn't wear clerical dress, just ordinary shirts and suits. There were no crosses in the church. No altar. No idolatry. No stained-glass windows. All these were sacrilege.

There was no set order of service and no ritual. The focal point was the pulpit and the sermon.

Catholics and Anglicans were considered evil. The Methodists were damned, and ordinary Baptists were heretical. We were exclusive, strict and particular and accepted everything by rote. We hated all forms of modernism. Even Billy Graham was considered too liberal for our taste. For that matter, so too was Ian Paisley!

We certainly didn't approve of football on Sundays and on that day our entertainment was protesting outside football grounds.

I found myself caught up in a kind of schizophrenic situation, being, on the one hand, a biblical fundamentalist and a critic of all other Christian groups and, on the other, not believing in anything. I wanted to believe but I couldn't. I just went along with the strict Baptist creed. I suppose I was indoctrinated, and the fact that I had been baptised and confirmed into the Catholic faith had become irrelevant. Unlike the local parish priest in Bolton: a chubby, twinkly-eyed and dedicated young enthusiast in a black suit, who would often call at Nanny's house in search of me, a missing member of his flock. Nanny, who had not approved of Catholics as a Salvationist, now saw them as outright devil-worshippers and would make me hide with her when the priest knocked on our front door. She would pull me down to the floor and we would squat or sit there, below the level of the window, until he gave up and went away.

But Nanny's religion never interfered with her television viewing. Her favourite programme was Peyton Place, and, though I doubt the pastor would have approved, she was an avid viewer of this and many other scandalous soaps. She adored Liberace on a Saturday evening.

It was at this rather confused stage in my early teens – I was now 13 – that a minor miracle occurred, one that was destined to change my whole life.

A new teacher was appointed at Knowl View, and put in charge of my class. The system, a misnomer if ever there was one, which operated there was that each class, of about 15 boys, had the same teacher for a full year. Theoretically, they would teach all subjects, but in practice they often taught none. There were no formal lessons, no tests, no assessments and no exams at Knowl View. The opinion of the authorities seemed to be that we were not worth educating. We were merely being kept off the streets – at least that was the intention – and put on hold until we were old enough to become assembly-line fodder.

Apart from weekly woodwork and metalwork classes, we were allowed to get on with exactly what we wanted, which included putting our feet up and sleeping if we so chose. The last thing that appeared to be expected of our teachers was that they should actually teach.

Then Stanley Thomas arrived, and for me everything changed. This was the man who would rouse my curiosity, stimulate in me an unstoppable quest for knowledge and teach me how to think. He was to be my reverse nemesis, the one who would erase the effect of all the bad things in my life and steer me towards eventual happiness and fulfilment.

Chapter Twenty-Seven

The arrival of Stanley Thomas was, for me, like the arrival of the Robin Williams character in *Dead Poets' Society*. It was a revelation and an awakening.

He had long blond hair and a moustache, wore 'flower-power' shirts in purple, yellow and pink, ties with vivid psychedelic colours, and his jackets were velvet or corduroy. His appearance and demeanour, like his sharp sense of humour and his crackling intelligence, were light years away from those of our dreary warder-like teachers. He even spoke differently from the others, with an extremely grand accent rather like Laurence Olivier's.

I took to him immediately – and he to me. I suppose I was as unique among the pupils as he was among the staff, and I think he recognised in me someone on whom he could work, a blank canvas.

The other kids, at least those who could communicate, seemed content with the idea of working in a factory all their lives. I was not. I was open to everything and anything and eager to question it all, and I think Mr Thomas found this both challenging and stimulating.

It was quite a shock for me to discover that this flamboyant character, then 41, was a Church of Wales Anglican priest, ordained in 1968, who was doing a master's degree in education. This was not information he revealed to other boys at the school, and I later learned that I was the only pupil who knew his real vocation.

He played classical music for us in the classroom and talked about Dickens and Shakespeare. None of us had ever encountered anybody quite like him before. Some of the skinheads believed he was gay, which he wasn't, and tried to wind him up. But he handled their crude bullying tactics with rich good humour and devastating repartee and they soon learned to leave him alone rather than be so effortlessly exposed to public ridicule.

Mr Thomas had his own little flat in the school, where he would smoke Gitanes and drink dry white wine, both pure evil according to my Baptist pastors. I can still remember the distinctive smell of tobacco and wine in his flat whenever I think back to those days; they were comforting smells and never seemed stale. He also burned long tapers of incense in little china holders.

There was a big couch in his living room, covered in a very elegant woven tapestry, and two small armchairs. There were two small coffee tables and two full bookshelves with other books piled on the floor alongside them. He had an amazing collection of classical records and a modern record player. The fitted carpet was beige with polka dots and on the walls, which were all white, hung large framed copies of modern art, including works by Picasso and Dali.

I would go to Mr Thomas's flat twice a week and sometimes more often. He loved to provoke me, smoking and drinking in front of me, even though he knew I ardently disapproved. What he was doing, of course, was challenging my intellect.

I would say, 'How can you be a Christian and drink?' and he would reply, 'Would you like one?'

When I scolded him and told him that he was a heretic and that Anglican priests were devils, he would laugh.

During one of our early discussions, he introduced the subject of Darwin and suggested I should read *The Origin of Species*. I told him that as a strict Baptist I adhered to the belief in Adam and Eve and that it would be considered a sin by my church just to read that book. Indeed, some members of that strange sect still believe that to this day.

'But how can you criticise without having read the argument?' he replied.

It sounds crazy, going from not wanting to read to reading Darwin, but that is exactly what happened.

I had learned to read with Mr Bleasdale and still had the capacity to read. I had simply chosen not to do so. I did have a fantastic memory, however, which I still have, and I had retained the ability to read. So, armed with a dictionary, I embarked on Darwin's masterpiece.

I loved the book. It opened my view of universality. I could see that everything was linked and that human life was evolving.

When Mr Thomas said, 'I think you need a drink,' I would reply, 'It's a sin to drink.'

'What about Jesus turning water into wine?'

'That was Ribena.'

'Try living.'

I was a strange oddball little character, mentally bound in a weird puritan world, and in his way he was as eccentric as me. That was why we became friends.

He talked to me about the poet William Blake and told me I could read him if I wished. The choice was mine. I loved Blake's poems and am still a committed fan to this day.

Then came Shakespeare, followed by Oscar Wilde and Dickens, and I found myself in a printed paradise. Reading all these strange things and trying to make sense of them, with Mr Thomas's help, was expanding my boundaries in giant leaps.

Over some 18 months, my political sympathies see-sawed from left to right, probably influenced by the books I was reading. At 15, I was slightly rebellious and had become an admirer of Harold Wilson, who, I was actually aware, was the current Labour opposition leader. But within months I had embraced communist ideology, and a few months later I had become a fascist.

Mr Thomas insisted I read Karl Marx and then introduced me to Hitler's *Mein Kampf*. I had no knowledge at all of the Second World War except from the RAF stories told me by my father, though he had not mentioned the Nazi leader's name. I told Mr Thomas that the world Hitler described sounded like a real Utopia, and now I was able to compare Hitler and Marx, and concluded they were rather alike in their methods of controlling people. I had read *Mein Kampf* with no agenda, so now Mr Thomas gave me *The Rise and Fall of the Third Reich* and biographies of Mussolini and Franco, which broadened my perspective on the fascist phenomenon in Europe.

Next I devoured Nietzsche, on whose thought Hitler had in part based his philosophy, and Wagner, whose monumental music had drawn inspiration from the same writings, and then started on thinkers such as Kierkegaard, Bertrand Russell and George Bernard Shaw.

At 15, in this crazy environment, surrounded by rent boys, drug dealers and the mentally subnormal, I had become something of a philosophic eccentric.

Under Mr Thomas's guidance, I also started to paint, and was allowed to join the sixth-form art class at a local secondary school. It taught me that there were normal people in the world who did not beat you up. They may have been older than me but I found that I could fit in, just as I had earlier on my school trip to Europe.

My painting also had a secondary benefit. It excused my participating in sport, which I loathed.

With a first name like mine, I fancied myself as something of a Michelangelo and over the next three years I painted a huge mural on a wall of the school dining hall, depicting Napoleon's retreat from Moscow. It was some 12 feet long by 6 feet high.

Amazingly, I became the only child in the history of that school to gain an O Level in any subject. It was in art.

I didn't appreciate it at the time, but what I was receiving from Mr Thomas was, to all intents and purposes, a private education, albeit one based on classical values. I've never understood 'modern' because I have had no training at all in anything technical, and I'm still frightened by technology.

But, for literature, theatre, music and art, Mr Thomas was my personal Professor Higgins; an immense genius. He took me to the theatre and concerts and art galleries – while my contemporaries were listening to the Beatles – and opened up worlds that I would otherwise never have known existed.

It was almost certainly because of all my new knowledge, and the enormous boost to my confidence it provided, that I was singled out by our new resident trainee social worker, Mary, who was only 19 and very pretty. She had a gorgeous figure and wore tight jeans and tops. I was not yet 16 and not much to look at, but that didn't matter. I was experiencing my very first crush, and went to sleep every night with thoughts of Mary wrapped in my arms.

The reality was far more mundane. We had regular discussion sessions, just the two of us, for she, like all her colleagues, had been told about my mother's suicide and my reluctance to take part in normal life, and I was, I suppose, an interesting subject for study. But I was no longer, I think she soon realised, the boy described in my thick bundle of case notes. Over the past two years, I had become a different person, and possibly her equal intellectually. I could discuss philosophy, theology, sociology, art and the theatre intelligently, knowledgeably and in great detail, which made me quite an oddity, considering my age and situation.

Perhaps she was just being kind, or more likely she simply wanted to show me off to her friends, but Mary invited me to spend the weekend with herself and her parents in Bristol, to meet some of her former school chums. Already secretly besotted with her, I jumped at the opportunity to spend a whole weekend in her company, hardly daring to think what it might lead to.

The headmaster and Nanny had to give their permission, and I think Nanny was quite nervous about me going off with a young woman for the weekend, but in the end they both agreed.

My first adult trip away from home provided some of the most fascinating days of my life up until that time, though sadly not in the way I had anticipated. Mary and her friends treated me as though I were their age – four or five years my senior – and I found I could talk with them as equals. We spent hours in coffee bars and restaurants discussing everything from the most unimportant trivia to deeply intellectual subjects and I revelled in being a part of it. They took me to the Bristol Old Vic and introduced me to my first-ever pizza.

Sadly, though, I gradually understood that Mary's interest in me was a mixture of professional and purely platonic. She may have found me an intellectual equal and a fascinating case study, but I was a non-starter as a potential boyfriend.

I thought, no doubt like millions of lovesick boys before me, that my heart would break, and I followed Mary around like an orphaned puppy for several weeks, but, in the end, time, as ever, proved a masterly healer and I was able to get over my unrequited love.

I may have conquered my infatuation for Mary but I still couldn't cope with salvation. I spent many nights praying for it, because the Baptist pastors kept telling me that if I wasn't saved I would surely go to hell. But what they called 'my conversion experience' never came. I knew I was supposed to allow Jesus to save me, but he obviously didn't feel so inclined. I felt absolutely excluded, and in the end I decided to pretend to be saved.

Still only 15, I asked to be baptised as, in the words of the faith, an 'exclusive, strict and particular' Baptist. As I stood before the congregation in Moses Gate

Baptist church in the Bolton suburb of Farnworth, I swore that I accepted and understood Jesus Christ as saviour and ruler of my life.

Mr Thomas came to witness the event and probably thought I was mad. I thought so too, and hoped that if Jesus did exist he would forgive me for lying about my beliefs. But at least I felt safe, and that I wouldn't go to hell any more. So it was definitely worth the deception.

This was also the time I rethought my plans for suicide.

Nanny would often say, 'I don't want to live any more. I wish the Lord would take me.' But then she would say that she had one good reason to go on living, and that was me. During my weekends at home with her, I would mow the lawn and do the other chores, but I was gradually becoming aware that I also had a deeper responsibility for my grandmother.

In addition, Mr Thomas's teaching had radically altered my perception of just about everything and I concluded, one evening as I lay on my bed, that I no longer wanted to kill myself. The world had become an infinitely more interesting place to be in. I wanted to stay.

Chapter Twenty-Eight

At the age of 16, after more than a decade of terror and turmoil, I finally entered a more tranquil period. At Knowl View, I had graduated from the shared dormitory to a room of my own and, though I was still in a state of considerable isolation, I had developed a satisfying and at times pleasing way of life.

Shortly before leaving Rochdale, I was told by one of the social workers there that some of the younger children, newly arrived at the school, modelled themselves on me because I followed a very diplomatic path, avoiding or deflecting potentially injurious encounters with fellow pupils.

I was very aware, intuitive and immensely sensitive, and was able to pick up others' vibes. But no warning antenna in the world could have prepared me for the traumatic revelation awaiting me in the headmaster's study when I was called there in the spring of 1974.

It was the month before my 17th birthday, and I was about to leave Knowl View to try to make my own way in the world – though not, I had promised myself, the way they had planned for me to go, in a factory.

Having assumed I was about to be given the standard school-leaver's pep talk, I was surprised to be told to sit down in the chair facing Mr Turner across his desk. We were normally made to stand, to receive our plaudits or punishments, after being summoned individually to the headmaster's study.

Mr Turner was a huge but very gentle man, and extremely kind, but on this occasion he looked uncharacteristically grim and seemed to be having difficulty knowing where to start. In the end, he must have decided to get it over with quickly, because he told me, in a sort of rush, that my grandmother had asked him to reveal to me some important details from my past. To tell me the truth – namely, that Joe and Lillian Seed had not been my real parents. They had adopted me from the Catholic Children's Society when I was about a year and a half old.

I'm rather glad I was sitting down when he dropped that bombshell. It actually took my breath away. I felt quite light-headed.

My real name, it appeared, was Steven Wayne Godwin and my mother had been a young mill worker called

Marie. My father was unknown. I had only become Michael Joseph Steven Wayne Seed, by adoption, on 11 November 1958, when I was 17 months old, having been baptised a Catholic in my real name by the Jesuits a year earlier, at the Holy Name Church in Oxford Road, Manchester.

I sat there speechless, barely able to think. All that cruelty and pain and heartbreak, and all of it had been based on a lie.

Mr Turner asked me if I understood and if I was all right.

I nodded. That was all I could manage.

'Your grandmother feels that you had a right to know this, but also feels that you may not want to go on seeing her. She's frightened that you may want to sever all ties with her as she is not your natural grandmother.'

I found this news even more distressing than the revelation that I was adopted. Nanny was the only person, to my knowledge, who had ever shown any affection towards me or claimed to have loved me. The thought of a future in which she did not play a part was very bleak indeed.

Mr Turner was looking at me expectantly.

I found I had to clear my voice a couple of times to speak. I told him, 'My parents are dead as far as I am concerned. They were my parents. I'm not interested in looking for any others. I had quite enough trouble with the last ones.'

I felt like the character in *The Importance of Being Earnest*.

'This is your certificate of adoption, and these are the details of your birth mother,' the headmaster told me.

Bits of paper that made a mockery of my life up until now.

Just like Nanny, I thought. An absolute realist. She understood that, leaving school to make my own way in the world, I might need proper identification. To know who I really was. She was still thinking of me and I loved her more than ever because of it.

And it was a real pleasure indeed to know that I was not related in any way to the Wicked Witch of the West.

'You've got a lot to think about, Michael,' said Mr Turner. 'And, if I might offer you some advice, I would say that it would be wise for you to think very carefully before embarking on any attempts to uncover your real family. All this must have come as quite a shock. Let this information I've given you today sink in properly before you do anything.'

I walked back to my room in a daze. Mr Turner's disclosures had been cataclysmic in their effect. They offered possible explanations of events that had seemed so senseless before.

My father's anger for one.

He had obviously blamed my mother for not being able to have babies, and not having a son to carry on his line must have festered in him. I realised then that many of his remarks had their origins in this. She was clearly not the wife he wanted.

After his marriage, he had been away, or abroad, until the end of the war, then did a series of jobs he didn't really like. I thought now that he must have seen himself as a failure, with no point to his life. His own depression, coupled with the alcohol, did the rest.

I could never excuse what he had done to me and I know that he drove my mother to suicide. It was as though he had murdered her. But I was as certain now as I could ever be that all their problems, and my mother's awful depression, probably had their roots in the 16 years they had tried, and failed, to have children of their own.

Then they had adopted me. But I wasn't his child. I was just nobody's child. A constant daily reminder of his inability to father a child of his own. I understood then the hatred and the anger and why I must eventually forgive him. But the memories were still too fresh to attempt that step then.

I explained this to Nanny when I went home that weekend. She was in tears when she opened the front door and pulled me into her arms. She had spent the whole week knowing Mr Turner was going to break the news and fearing that she would never see me again.

I kissed her on both soft cheeks, which were wet with her tears, and hugged her again and told her she was the loveliest nanny any boy could ever wish for, and that I would always love her and need her. And she told me I was the best grandson in the world and she was so proud of me.

227

It didn't matter to either of us who my real parents were. Our bond was still there, and that was all that counted.

Chapter Twenty-Nine

Nanny was to remain a constant in my life until she died 20 years later, at the age of 94. But my feelings towards my parents had been irrevocably altered.

I still grieved for Mammy and loved her just as much as before, but I felt a growing resentment towards her for not having told me the truth about my birth before she killed herself. It would probably not have made the pain any easier to bear, but it just might have stopped me blaming myself for her suicide.

I had instinctively felt my father was a stranger when he forced me to perform those disgusting sexual services, and knowing now that I had been right could never erase the memories. But at least it was some comfort to learn that it had not been my real father making me participate in such unnatural acts.

I never did find out who my real father was, and I had – and still have – no desire to seek him out.

But within a year of discovering my true identity I met Sister Philomena, the nun who had handled my adoption, and she told me the sad story of the young Irish girl, my mother, who came to England to have her baby, and loved him so much she had to give him away.

Marie Godwin was only 16 when she became pregnant, Sister Philomena told me, and had to leave home in Ireland to save herself and her family from the shame of having an illegitimate child. She was a mill worker, but found herself a job in nursing at a hospital in Manchester.

I was born on Sunday, 16 June 1957 in Gore Street and was registered as birth number 396 in the sub-district of Manchester Western. My father's name was left blank on the birth certificate.

Sister Philomena said that Marie, who was very pretty and had dark curly hair and a ready, sunny smile, loved me very much and looked after me herself for more than six months, having me baptised a Catholic in December that year.

But, even though she was working, Marie found she could not provide adequate food, clothing and care for me, and eventually the financial strain proved too much.

'In January of 1958 she brought you to me, at the Catholic Children's Society in Salford, and asked if we could find you good parents who could give you a decent start in life,' the nun told me. 'Marie kept in touch with me for a year, until after you were safely adopted, in November 1958, because she wanted to know about the couple who would be raising you. What kind of people they were. She hated giving you away because she loved you so much. But that was all she could offer. Her love. She thought you deserved more.'

I cried then, deep sobs that seemed to come from the bottom of my soul. All I had ever craved, as long as I could remember, was to be loved. Nothing more.

It may have been all she could give – but it was everything I had ever wanted, and I cried for us both, for all the love the two of us had lost. As I clung to Sister Philomena, with tears pouring down my face, I mourned for those might-have-been years, when there could have been so many beautiful dreams, instead of all the frightful nightmares.

Sister Philomena said that my mother had stayed in touch with her until the month after I was adopted, to make sure I was in safe hands; and after that she never heard from Marie again.

I later discovered that Joe and Lillian Seed had adopted another baby boy at the same time as me but within a few weeks had sent him back to the Catholic Children's Society.

In those days, before the age of computers, all the records were written or typed and those at the Society had been destroyed by fire. There was no record of why the other baby had been returned. Nanny either genuinely didn't know or remember, or she may have professed ignorance to protect her daughter, and I never saw the Wicked Witch of the West again to ask her.

Whatever the reason, it might have lost me a childhood companion, but almost certainly saved that child from the most awful pain and some very unpleasant moments. I hope that child was adopted by a couple who loved and cared for their baby in the way that every child should be loved and cared for.

How different my life might have been if I had been the one to have been rejected.

Chapter Thirty

I left school in May 1974, the year of my 17th birthday, with one O Level in art, a wide knowledge of politics, economics, philosophy and the theatre, and a total ignorance of technology, mechanics, electricity and simple arithmetic.

Britain was still recovering from the disastrous three-day working week brought in by Ted Heath, which had cost him the next general election, and jobs were hard to come by.

But I was lucky. A job was advertised in the *Bolton Evening News* for a helper in Knutsford motorway cafe, and after being interviewed on the telephone I was offered a try-out on a day-to-day basis.

The job mainly involved collecting plates, cutlery and trays from the restaurant and taking them to the kitchen to be washed up. I was also detailed to help with certain chores in the kitchen itself.

On my first day, I managed to drop a tray holding more than 60 eggs on the kitchen floor and smash the lot. Reluctantly, the management agreed to have me back the following day, but it proved to be a big mistake on their part. This time I slipped on the kitchen floor, knocked over a trolley and smashed nearly a hundred plates, cups and saucers that were stored on it.

I was fired on the spot, given two pound notes and a handful of silver coins for the total of ten hours I had worked there and told never to come back.

But luck was still with me. Walking along the High Street, I spotted a handwritten sign in the window of a menswear shop which said, 'Help needed inside.' They wanted an assistant salesman, and after a five-minute interview I was given the job.

For a time all went well, and except for my boss not approving of my telling customers that they could buy similar clothing more cheaply at other shops in town, I seemed to be getting on quite well.

Until the day they asked me to make the tea.

Call it bizarre if you like, but there was one problem with this. I had never made a cup of tea or paid attention to one being made in my life. Nanny put her lovely complexion down to drinking only orange juice or milk, and I drank only orange juice or water. At school, I was never shown, or asked, to put the kettle on, and at home my grandmother did all that.

I managed to fill the kettle all right, and spotted that it had a wire coming out of it with a plug on the end. So I plugged it in. And to be on the safe side, because I vaguely remembered my grandmother doing it, I lit the gas on top of the stove and put the kettle on top of that.

After a few minutes, I noticed that the plastic part of the kettle was on fire, but, before I could rescue it, the whole thing blew up with an almighty bang and sent bits of plastic flying everywhere.

All the lights went out in the kitchen and in the shop, and as I had no idea of the existence of such things as fuses and fuse boxes, I didn't know what to do.

They had heard the bang in the shop downstairs and then been plunged into darkness. Now one of the men came running upstairs to see what had happened.

I was so scared I hid behind the door, but my fellow assistant found me and hauled me downstairs, where the boss, shouting at the top of his voice, demanded to know what the hell was going on.

When I explained, he could scarcely believe me.

'I didn't know anybody could be that bloody thick,' he stormed. 'This definitely isn't going to work out. You're fired.'

I had been there exactly two weeks.

My next job was as a care worker for the mentally ill in a centre run by Bolton Social Services – whose care I was still in myself.

To qualify for care, the patients had to be

ambulatory and not physically impaired, just mentally ill. There were about 30 male residents in the nursing home. Some were middle-aged but most of them were elderly.

The people looking after them were a married couple, John and Irene Osborne, who were really nice. They had a daughter, Karen, and a son, Paul, who were both still at school. They were amazingly funny and quite outrageous and, with the exception of Mr Thomas, very different from most of the people I knew. We were surrounded by dysfunctional, pretty crazy residents, but that didn't stop us having the most enormous fun, and soon I learned to accept the madness around us as quite normal.

One old man used to throw handfuls of his own faeces at people in the street from an upstairs window, and the majority of them were unpredictable, but we coped. There were just the Osbornes, two ladies and me. We did everything.

I had to help in the kitchen and with the cleaning, and one of my regular tasks was to make sure that everyone got out of bed in the morning. Some of them never wanted to get up, and it often took a lot of tugging, pushing and persuasion to get them on the move. At 17, I had to take the initiative and provide a lead. I'm not so sure one could get away with using a 17-year-old to do the job today. But I was in my element.

One resident, an old rag-and-bone man, who parked his cart at the back of the home, refused to ever wash his hands, so by the front door we kept a pair of white opera gloves and he was made to put these on when he came home from work.

When one evening I was slightly delayed serving his dinner, he took a pair of goldfish out of the tank in the living room, placed them between two slices of bread and ate them alive.

None of the other residents found this the slightest bit unusual. It was that kind of place.

Some of them didn't really know how to look after themselves, and I found that in assisting them I was satisfying a need in myself to help others. At this point, I began to think seriously about a career in the social services.

I stayed with the Osbornes for a year and a half, living with my grandmother and walking to and from work every day. Nearly every day, I would be accosted by three teenage girls, some of my worst persecutors, screaming abuse and obscenities. I began to believe that there would never be an end to this kind of thing. It was so depressing. I desperately needed an enormous uplift, both humanly and spiritually.

By now, I had moved on from the Baptists, much to Nanny's disgust, and for a brief time attended an Anglican church. But eventually, and I suppose inevitably, because of my background, I returned to the Catholic Church.

I was aware too that, of the thousands of religious orders that exist, most of them are Catholic, and though other religions treat most of these orders as oddities, the

Catholic religion considers them quite normal. That also appealed to me. I approved of a religion that found these supposed oddities normal, just as I found normal the odd characters in the nursing home where I worked.

I had read GK Chesterton's *St Francis of Assisi* and gradually my desire to help other people began to merge with the idea of becoming a friar.

I could have gone on working for the Osbornes for another five years and gained the work experience to help run a similar home myself, but by then the call of Catholicism was already too strong to ignore. And, on a tragic note, John Osborne died at that time, shortly followed by his wife.

In September 1975, I left the home for crazy people and started work at a Catholic hostel for the homeless in the centre of Manchester. To my surprise and relief, they had accepted me without credentials. They regarded my work there as a test for me before entering a seminary.

As the result of this successful tryout, in January the following year, as human and sinful as I am, I committed myself irrevocably to a life of service under God and took the first step which would eventually lead to my becoming a friar in the Franciscan Order.

Postscript

The Reverend Stanley Thomas remained a close friend of Father Michael Seed until his death on 7 March this year. After leaving Knowl View School in 1979, where he had become Deputy Headmaster, he became vicar of a small parish church in Wales before retiring. He was 75.

Nanny Mary 'Polly' Ramsden moved to a controlled bungalow for the elderly in the centre of Bolton when Michael left home in 1975, and lived there until 1986, when she entered The Little Sisters of the Poor nursing home in Leeds. After a lifetime committed to the Salvation Army and the Baptists she died there, two years later, aged 94, as a Roman Catholic.

Florence Seed, the 'Wicked Witch of the West', died in December 1977, aged 85. She is buried, with her husband, two sons and daughter, Sheila, who died in 2003 aged 79, in a shared grave in Allerton Cemetery, near Halewood.

The ashes of Lillian Seed, Father Michael's mother, rest in Bolton, 25 miles from the Seed family plot in Halewood: as separated in death from her husband Joe as she was during their marriage.

In September 2002, David Higgins, 62, was jailed for 12 months in Manchester after admitting he had preyed on children while working and living at Knowl View School in Rochdale, where, the court was told, he was regarded as a father figure to the boys, who came from troubled backgrounds. He pleaded guilty to 11 counts of indecent assault and gross indecency with a child. The pupils who gave evidence had been at the school in the early 1970s and came forward after the launch of Operation Cleopatra, Greater Manchester Police's biggest-ever investigation into child abuse in residential homes, which began in 1997. He was banned from working with children for life and ordered to sign the Sex Offenders' Register.

Higgins had two other convictions for indecently assaulting children. In 1976, in Leeds he had been given a 12-month conditional discharge, and in Skipton in 1983 he was placed under two years' probation. Both courts had been unaware of his activities at Knowl View.

Knowl View Special School for Emotionally and Behaviourally Disturbed Children remained operational for 21 years after Michael Seed left. It was partially burned down by its then pupils and was shut down by Rochdale Council in 1995 amid allegations of sexual abuse and mismanagement.

Epilogue

Though the story of my childhood ended when I was 17, the story of my road to manhood and my chosen vocation within the Catholic Church had only just begun.

It was not a simple route I took. In fact, my journey towards God was rather like navigating a three-dimensional maze of mirrors with a constantly moving centre.

It was a fascinating journey, full of wonderful characters, often funny, sometimes difficult and occasionally quite terrifying. As in any great maze, there were dead ends and false trails and tempting openings to lure me in the wrong direction.

But I never lost my belief that it was God who was guiding my footsteps and that, if I listened to Him, I must ultimately arrive at the right destination.

My first steps towards God were faltering and uncertain. I did not know even if I was heading in the right direction. I was still only 17 and working in the nursing home in Bolton when I made my first moves towards breaking with the strict and particular Baptists. I had experienced the heavy influences of liberalism and universality and no longer wanted to belong to a tiny and exclusive sect.

Mr Thomas, my teacher at Knowl View School, had broadened my concepts and I had begun to develop a stronger faith as a Christian. But I needed to find some expression and wasn't sure where to direct it, and in my search I turned first to the Anglican Church.

The obvious choice was Bolton Parish Church, which was close to where we lived, but when I walked in I was completely overwhelmed. It is an enormous church, about the size of Canterbury Cathedral, and I found it almost frightening.

Much better, I thought, to ease my way in with something more manageable and I plumped for St Paul's, a smaller church conveniently sited by the main bus stop in Bolton market. St Paul's was deeply evangelical, which was extremely Low Church, and fitted well with the traditions I had already adopted from the Salvation Army and the Baptists.

Canon Colin Craston was a committed Low Church

man and one of the leaders of the evangelical tradition in Britain. A tough, uncompromising man. At least, sadly, that's the way he came across to me.

After my first visit to St Paul's I asked if we could talk and he sat me down there and then in a pew and told me to say my piece. My account of my somewhat complex religious background, which ended with my baptism, by full immersion, into the Baptist Church, took me almost an hour, and he listened patiently, in silence, until I had finished.

His first comment took me completely by surprise. 'You, Michael, are a Catholic.'

I said, 'I'm certainly not. Catholics aren't Christians.'

I noticed he didn't bother to disagree with this statement, but he repeated, 'You are a Catholic. Were you baptised?'

'Yes,' I replied. 'I now understand that I was baptised a Catholic as a baby.'

'Well, you're a Catholic then.'

I reminded him I had been baptised a Baptist when I was 15. Didn't that cancel out what had happened to me as a baby?

'No,' he told me. 'You're definitely still a Catholic.'

'I know what I am and it's not that,' I insisted. 'I really don't care what you think I am, but what I want to be is a member of the Church of England.'

Strangely, had it not been for that mad conversation with Canon Craston, I would not have actually considered universality in the sense that the word 'Catholic' means universal. One evening that week, and in the week that followed, he insisted on my spending time at his residence, listening to him expound on the differences between Catholics and Anglicans. It made not a scrap of difference to him how much I protested that this wasn't necessary. That I had been considering becoming a Baptist pastor and had attended Bible College at Birkenhead on several weekends with that aim in mind.

'I am an evangelical,' I kept telling him. 'I am not a Catholic, so why are you wasting our time giving me all the differences?'

The result of these lectures was really hilarious. He hammered home the differences between the two churches so convincingly that I ended up thinking to myself, My God, the Catholic Church actually appears more attractive.

But by this time the good canon had determined that I should be formally received into his church in the middle of Evensong, to publicly recant my belief in the Catholic Church.

'You will have to denounce the heresies of the Church of Rome in front of the whole congregation,' he said.

I was as nervous as any other 17-year-old and I certainly didn't want to let him down, but I had to protest. 'I've already told you that I'm not a Catholic and I don't really want to renounce being what I'm not, either privately or publicly.'

'You were baptised as a baby and you have to do it,' he said.

I suddenly realised that, to him, my conversion had become a political as well as a personal issue. I couldn't conceive that any Roman Catholic in Bolton had ever renounced his faith publicly and become an Anglican. This wasn't a normal happening. It was more like something out of Oliver Cromwell's times.

At this point, I had decided that I didn't want to go through with the ceremony. But I did it anyway – out of fear. I also had a horror of letting people down.

Nor were my fears eased by the reaction of my local Baptist pastor when I told him I was about to join the Church of England.

'You will be leading souls to hell if you become an Anglican,' he warned me.

The thought flashed into my mind: perhaps I had better go for gold and become a Catholic, then I can really lead them to hell.

On that dreadful Sunday when Canon Craston called me forward to the altar, I felt that I was walking towards a gallows. He had a whole list of things I had to denounce, half of which I didn't totally understand the meaning of.

'Do you denounce the teachings of Rome, which are contrary to Scripture?'

'I do.'

'Do you abhor belief in Mary?'

'I do.'

On and on it went, until finally he welcomed me into the Church of England.

When it was all over, I was doubly certain that I did not want to remain an Anglican. If this was the Church of England, I wanted none of it.

Ironically, though, it was his trying to make me an Anglican which brought me back to the Catholic Church.

In the midst of all this nonsense, I felt I had to talk to someone else about what was happening. I continued attending St Paul's for two more Sundays.

Instead, I plucked up my courage and went to a service at St Peter's, the vast and intimidating parish church, and there I met the lovely, almost saintly Reverend Sydney Clayton, who turned out to be Stanley Thomas's intellectual double. He was a progressive Anglican and really rather grand, and was the number two at St Peter's.

There was an archdeacon in charge, and below him Sydney, who had the marvellously puritan title of 'lecturer'. There are only six church lecturers in England. The posts were created by Cromwell and the lecturer's job was to stand in the market squares of his certain towns and preach a puritanical Protestant sermon once a year. That, and to correct heresy. Bolton was one of the original six towns to have a lecturer assigned to it.

Sydney Leigh Clayton was an academic and treated the traditional duty that went with his title as something of a joke, though it did have an income attached to it.

The similarities between Stanley and Sydney were remarkable. The first had proved an angel at Knowl

View, and had looked after me when I was lost and abandoned as a teenager. Now, when I was feeling spiritually lost in Bolton and not certain of my future, there was Sydney Clayton.

He was a very holy person. Gentle, erudite and precise and very friendly, he worked as an examiner for the University of London's BA degree in Divinity. He also marked O- and A-Level papers.

When I first met Sydney Clayton, he was in his mid-thirties and had sparse, swept-back hair and very white skin. Even though it was the 1970s, he always dressed in very correct Edwardian style and wore a full white-cotton dog collar. He had been educated at Lincoln Theological College, which has a Low Church, broad-minded evangelical tradition, and was a Pembroke College, Oxford classical scholar, an expert in Greek, Hebrew and Latin. A serious academic, but one of the least pretentious people I have ever met.

Following our first meeting, Sydney Clayton invited me to his residence and again I was asked to recount the whole of my religious background. Afterwards, he told me, 'Don't worry about anything. The job of the Church is to be welcoming. It's for everybody. But in a funny way perhaps Colin Craston could be right. The Catholics are wonderful people, you know. Maybe it is correct for you to become a Catholic.'

'Maybe,' I replied. 'But I have this strong urge to join a community – perhaps because I haven't had a proper family in my life. I'd like to become a monk.'

He didn't know much about monks at all, he said. 'They are a kind of strange group in the Church of England, and there are not many of them. They are tiny and slightly freaky,' he said. I think he was amused by them in a kindly way. 'They'll probably rename you Brother Fred,' he laughed. 'But by all means write to them.'

He gave me a list of addresses and I wrote to them all, and they all replied. But only one group asked me to visit, and none of them said I could enter. They all felt that at 17 I was too young to make such a commitment.

In response to their letter, I went by coach to Ewell Monastery in Kent, an Anglican Cistercian brotherhood which had been founded in 1966 on a six-acre site close to the village of West Malling. It was all worship and prayer, work and study, and they lived under a very strict regime, almost like silent monks. If I was interested in joining them, I was told, I should get back in touch when I was three years older.

I wasn't.

'Well,' said Sydney Clayton, 'perhaps it's time to think again about going back to the Catholic Church. Everything is much more friendly between us these days. We get on very well with one another now. And there is a lot more variety and expression of the kind of thing you are looking for in the Catholic Church. That is where nearly all the religious orders come from. St Francis and St Benedict and the like are all Catholic. I think it's time you gave the Catholics another chance.'

It was the push I needed.

My first Mass as an adult was in a church next door to a pub, in a very Irish part of Bolton. I went on a Saturday evening and my first impression was that it reeked of alcohol. At six o'clock, they all appeared to be drunk — and happy. The Catholics clearly welcomed sinners as well as saints — and that made it perfect for me.

The priest preached only briefly and was dull and boring, and looked a bit of an old grump, but I enjoyed the silent bits and the mystery. And by the end of that service I felt strongly that I had to talk to a Catholic priest. God, I believed, had led me to Sydney Clayton, and he, in turn, had guided me to this place.

I must have stood on his doorstep for several minutes working up enough courage to ring the bell, but eventually I did, and moments later Father John Ashworth opened the door.

I immediately launched into the story of my life and he held up both hands, palms towards me, in a calming gesture. 'Listen to me,' he said. 'Whoever you are, I think you need a drink.'

He led me through to a little parlour and told me to sit down while he poured me a glass of what I later learned was sweet white Vermouth. It had a very odd taste, but in those days I was virtually a stranger to alcohol of any description and had no idea what anything should taste like. Occasionally I had sipped a little white wine with Mr Thomas, but that was the full extent of my drinking experience.

Once he was satisfied that I was settled, Father John

invited me to tell my story. He nodded gently from time to time and when I had finished he smiled at me and said, 'I think we can sort you out. There is nothing really to talk about. You're a Catholic. It's as simple as that, and I'll show you why.'

He reached into a drawer and brought out a copy of the Penny Catechism, a catechism being a set of questions and answers on religious doctrine. The Penny Catechism contains a hundred or more questions and answers and is very ancient. It is a childlike document but very popular, and Catholics all over the world have been raised on it. There is nothing like it, though a sign of the changing times is that the Penny Catechism now costs £3.

The first question is: 'Who made me?'

Answer: 'God made me.'

Question: 'Why did He make me?'

Answer: 'To know Him, love Him and serve Him.'

We went through every question and in the end Father John asked me, 'Is there anything there you disagree with, or have a problem with?'

I shook my head. As we had worked our way through the catechism, I had started to remember it from my childhood at St Osmund's Primary School. We had learned a lot of it by rote, and now it came flooding back.

Father John became a good friend and counsellor. He was a typical, no-nonsense, old-fashioned Lancashire Catholic priest.

After a couple more sessions in his parlour, with the

white Vermouth, he said to me, 'Michael, all I have to do with you now is to hear your confession. I know you've done that as a child but we need to do it again now to restore you fully to Mother Church.'

I thought he would hear my confession there and then, in his parlour, but he said, 'No.'

He put on his full robes and adornments and led me to the church, which he had to unlock, switched on the lights and took his place inside the little confession box.

I had to kneel down on the other side of the screen, as though I didn't know who he was, and make my confession.

Afterwards, we turned off the lights, locked the church and returned to his parlour.

I learned later that this was so typical of Father John. He was so wonderfully formal. Very orthodox. Very traditional. Very proper. He didn't like anything liberal.

We got on very well.

My re-embracing of the Catholic faith officially ended my membership of the Anglican Church, which had lasted exactly three months, and, though I continued my friendship with Sydney Clayton, I never again spoke to Canon Craston. He was a man highly respected in evangelical circles but, because of his uncompromising attitude, was not always popular with his parishioners.

During our regular chats, I had told Father John of my thoughts of becoming a priest or a monk. Like Sydney Clayton, he did not relate too well to monks, but he urged me to seriously consider becoming a priest. They needed priests in the diocese, he said.

I was very happy with his guidance and decided to telephone the Salford diocesan recruiter to arrange a meeting.

There was a local *Catholic Directory* in the nursing home, which the goldfish-eating rag-and-bone man had brought back from one of his daily scavenges, and I searched in there for the number I needed. I wanted the Diocesan Director of Vocations to the priesthood. Inevitably, being me, I picked out the wrong number and found myself speaking to Father Tony Grimshaw, the Diocesan Director of Missions, who arranged to come round and see me.

We met in Nanny's house, and it says a lot for Father Tony's charm and personality that she actually offered him refreshments while he was there. She had been disgusted by my switch to the Anglicans and almost speechless when I announced my return to the despised Catholics, and for her to welcome one of the 'enemy' into her home was a rare favour.

Father Tony, it turned out, was a Diocesan priest in Manchester who was on loan to the African missions by the Bishop of Salford. He was in his mid-thirties but looked to be still in his early twenties, dashing, energetic and full of enthusiasm. He was a truly dynamic character, very good-looking and with longish, blond hair. His uncle was the Archbishop of Birmingham.

Father Tony explained that he had just come back

from a mission in Africa and that they were in urgent need of priests out there.

'What about priests here?' I asked.

'We have plenty of priests here,' he assured me. 'What we really need are priests in Africa. That's what you should think about.'

I hit it off with Father Tony from the outset, and he introduced me to a special Sunday-evening prayer meeting for priests which took place at about eight o'clock, after the usual services, in a church in Bolton run by an enormous man called Monsignor John O'Connor.

There were about 15 priests and me and we would have extemporaneous prayers and sing a few songs. It was not typically Catholic, for we were what is called 'charismatic'. This was a style which originated in the Pentecostal churches. Happy-clappy, they call it now, and it is very like the black churches in America. This charismatic movement had come into the Catholic Church in the late 1960s.

I had gone from not knowing any Catholic priests to being part of a regular prayer meeting with a whole group of them. After prayers, we would have something to eat and drink and chat to one another. I was extremely happy to be one of them and found I was gradually, and contentedly, becoming more and more deeply immersed in my newly rediscovered religion.

Towards the end of that summer of 1975, shortly after I had turned 18, Tony introduced me to the vocational director, or recruiter, for a French religious order called the Society of African Missions (Sociètè des Missionnaires d'Afrique). In Britain, the SMA's members were nearly all Irish priests and the recruiter, Father Denis O'Driscoll SMA, came from Cork.

We met in a Bolton pub and, amazingly, he accepted me on the spot.

'I'm sure you'll be fine,' he said. 'But you have only just become a Catholic and I want to make absolutely certain this is right for you. We'll try you out in Manchester at the centre for the homeless and the very needy and see how you get on. Our British headquarters is almost next door, so we'll be able to stay in touch and keep an eye on you. Consider this a sort of preparation.'

So that is how I came to leave my job at the nursing home and join the Morning Star Hostel in Manchester.

Things were moving fast. Too fast perhaps. I was a bit nervous of ending up defenceless in the centre of Africa, surrounded by savagery, snakes and man-eating wild animals.

For my peace of mind, I telephoned the man I had intended to call at the outset, Father Kevin Kenny, Director of Vocations for the Diocese of Salford.

Father Kevin, a traditional priest who always wore a full cassock, was secretary to, and lived in the residence of, the Bishop of Salford, the same one who had confirmed me as a child. I visited Father Kevin there in the Bishop's House, Wardley Hall, a beautiful Tudor house, and he agreed to help and counsel me if ever I felt the need.

Confident of his support if needed, and encouraged by my prayer-meeting priests in Bolton, I entered the Morning Star Hostel in Nelson Street, Manchester, just a few yards away from the Holy Name Church, where my real mother had taken me to be baptised. Now I found myself going there every Sunday for Mass. It was very odd, almost déja vu. Why, of all places in the world, should I find myself going there for Mass?

It was in Manchester that I met, for the first time, other young men who were about to train for the priesthood. Two young Jesuits were also working in the hostel and we became good friends.

The hostel was a desperate place, run by a lay Catholic movement called the Legion of Mary. They operate nationwide, wherever you find the most vulnerable, the needy and the poorest people. The Legion take collections for them and support them, and in some cases, such as the Morning Star Hostel, provided a shelter run by legionnaires.

It was my first introduction to a formal life. The day would begin at six o'clock with special prayers, followed by meditation and Mass and then breakfast. Some of the homeless would join us for one or more of these sessions.

Then came the work. I helped in the kitchen preparing food or washing up, then in the laundry or changing beds, setting tables, mopping floors or cleaning toilets. I had to be ready to turn my hand to whatever was needed.

There was a big dormitory for the homeless and a large dining hall and everywhere was kept immaculately clean. It was very hard work but somehow we managed to keep the hostel and the residents looking spotless.

The University of Manchester was directly opposite the hostel and some of the undergraduates volunteered to help. One of my jobs was to explain to them what to do. I found myself mixing with a group of serious intellectuals and didn't feel at all inadequate. Far from it. On some subjects, I even found I knew far more than them.

I would go to a special weekly Mass held in the chaplaincy of the University, presided over by some very trendy priests, and the students believed I was one of them. They saw no difference and I felt their equal. These were heady times for me.

They would talk of Descartes, Kierkegaard, Nietzsche and Wittgenstein and I could converse on them all knowledgeably and often with far more understanding and a deeper interpretation of their philosophies.

I was also expected to know a great deal about the Catholic Church, which was difficult as I had only just become a member. I carried dozens of scribbled notes in my pockets and somehow I managed to get through. I am ashamed to say, though, that occasionally I made up the answers.

I was expected to say the Rosary every night, and I didn't even know the Rosary. Some nights I was charged with reading the prayers and even had trouble with that. A rummage through my notes usually provided an answer of sorts.

That three-month period between September and Christmas was one of the happiest I can remember. The work was manual and didn't involve any thinking and I had nothing at all to worry about.

My excitement at being told, early in December, that I had been accepted by the Society of African Missions as a candidate and would be starting on a pre-seminary course at college in January was also tinged with regret to be leaving such a happy environment as the Morning Star Hostel.

St Mary's College was in Aberystwyth, halfway up the west coast of Wales on Cardigan Bay. It was run by Carmelite friars who wear the full habit with hood. Many of the Catholic orders and some of the dioceses send their students there if they feel they need a certain amount of preparation before entering a seminary. Some students were there for one or even two years, others for just a term or two.

The man in charge of the college was Father Prior Flanagan, an absolutely ferocious Irishman, known to everyone as 'Spuds', and I think he was wary of me from the start because he didn't consider me a proper Catholic.

One of the first students I palled up with was Alan, a graduate who was enrolled for a year to do further studies. He was a former strict Welsh Baptist and as an ex-Baptist myself we hit it off tremendously and quickly became the best of friends.

Our friendship was soon noted by the Prior Flanagan and he summoned me to his office.

'You are not to associate with Alan,' he told me bluntly. 'He is not a proper Catholic and you are not a proper Catholic, so you must not associate. You must only associate with proper Catholics who have been Catholics all their lives.'

If I disobeyed him, he said, he would throw me out.

It was an irresistible challenge to both Alan and I, and we continued to meet secretly in various parts of town. We shared an interest in other denominational churches and visited most of them in Aberystwyth. College rules insisted we wear cassocks most of the time, so it was virtually impossible to make ourselves invisible, even in a crowd.

Alan was slightly eccentric and suggested we leave little medals of Mary, called 'Miraculous Medals', in the fonts, pulpits and pews of all the churches we visited, partly as a calling card and partly in the slight hope that we might convert their congregations. It was wonderful, harmless fun.

We also used to enjoy a drink in the local pubs and would often be late back to college after the doors were locked. But even in our cassocks it was not difficult to climb in through one of the windows and we became very adept at sneaking in and out after dark.

Alan is now a highly respected monk and I am a friar,

but in those days in 1976 we were just two silly young people doing the kind of silly things young people have done for centuries.

It was inevitable, of course, that someone from college would spot us together and report us to the Father Prior, and that is exactly what happened.

Father Flanagan was almost apoplectic with rage. He ranted and raved at me for a good 15 minutes and I felt like a little schoolboy back in primary school, expecting him at any moment to produce a cane and command me to bend over.

He did write a letter of complaint to the Mission directors in Manchester, but in their kind wisdom they chose to take no further action. I do believe, though, that they, and certainly Father Flanagan, did not approve of my dabbling with other orders.

During the Easter break at Aberystwyth, I arranged to stay with the Dominican friars in Oxford for a week. I had met a Dominican priest who was also residing at St Mary's College and his stories had roused my interest in his order.

In Oxford, I met Father Timothy Radcliffe, then in his early thirties, who went on to be world leader of the Dominicans. He was even then a dynamic, charismatic figure and seemed to carry his destiny for greatness like an aura around him.

I made tentative suggestions about my becoming a Dominican friar and the Novice Master told me in a kindly but firm response that I didn't have enough studies behind me. The Dominicans are very big on studies and are all deeply intellectual.

But I enjoyed my week there and my contact with some of the young novices and it prompted me to dabble further into other orders.

Within the month, I had arranged to spend a weekend at the Birmingham Oratory, a Catholic community founded by Cardinal John Henry Newman in homage to St Philip Neri, whose first Oratory community was established in Italy in the 16th century.

I was desperate to find something I felt really called to. Although I was being sponsored by the Society of African Missions, I was still very uncertain if missionary work was the right vocation.

After Father Flanagan discovered about my dabbling and reported me to the SMA, I once more feared the worst. But again they decided to keep me.

Another student at Aberystwyth with whom I formed a lasting friendship was John Griffiths, who invited me to spend holidays with his family in South Wales and would remain my friend for 31 years. He is now a canon in the diocese of Cardiff.

Surprisingly, at the end of my first term, the SMA declared they were so pleased with my results and progress that they had decided to accelerate my entry into the novitiate. I would start as a novice in Ireland in September.

To our mutual delight, I was able to spend the summer with my grandmother, who had, by this time, moved to a controlled bungalow for the elderly in the middle of Bolton. She had become reconciled to my switch to Catholicism and was even beginning to show an interest in the religion. But, meanwhile, she continued to attend services with the Strict and Particular Baptists and, at the age of 82, was still turning out to protest against Sunday football matches and other such sins against the Sabbath.

I spent my last night in the UK with John Griffiths and his family in Aberdare and he drove me to Swansea docks the next morning to catch my boat to Cork.

The novitiate house was about a mile and a half from the centre of Cork. It looked very intimidating and austere – and very formal. Even the nuns who looked after us were strict. The place scared me at first.

We were put in large double bedrooms, each containing two single beds, two small wardrobes and a small bedside table and chair. The walls were painted white and the floors were scrubbed wooden boards with a few little mats scattered about on them. Everywhere was scrupulously clean.

To begin with, I walked about as though on eggshells, frightened of doing or saying the wrong thing. But, after a few days, I began to relax, and within a week I was beginning to enjoy myself.

The novitiate is the period, usually a year, during which a novice or prospective member of a religious order, who has not yet been admitted to vows, has to undergo training in order to be found eligible or qualified for admission. It is a very ancient tradition dating back to at least the 5th century.

One requirement of the students was that we had to work with local needy people. I was assigned to the psychiatric hospital and went there every Sunday to help out. I found I related to the inmates very well, because after my job in the nursing home in Bolton I was used to dealing with crazy people.

We were also obliged to join a society, and I was assigned to the Legion of Mary, with which I was very familiar. This one was based in the University of Cork, which allowed me, once again, to integrate with undergraduates. I was 19 and the students were mostly about the same age. One night a week, I was allowed to go to the Legion meeting and afterwards we would go out to the pub, and I usually managed to miss the last bus back to the novitiate.

My drink of choice had become Guinness, but one night I accompanied a group of students to a Republican get-together where a small barrel of poteen, illegally distilled Irish whiskey, was produced. It is like drinking liquid fire and rapidly affects your ability to do the simplest things. I drank it only the once and swore I would never touch it again. It took me days to recover.

Cork was a lot of fun and it wasn't uncommon, before we made our promises or vows, for students to form attachments with the young women of the town. I think it was even considered a challenge among some of the

Cork lasses to steal a novice student. And several of them were stolen successfully.

We did all sorts of silly things then and I was no exception. There was one young woman who seemed very keen on me. So keen, in fact, that she would walk me back to the novitiate after the pub closed, knowing that she would have to walk back alone into the centre of Cork afterwards.

Sweet kisses and loving endearments were exchanged but I think we both realised that the relationship could never lead to anything other than friendship.

Climbing in through the windows late at night had again become a way of life. But I have no regrets. It was a time of innocent adventure, with fun-filled days and nights providing many sweet and lasting memories, and I was extremely sad when the time came to leave.

I finished my novitiate and made my vows, or missionary promise, on my twentieth birthday, 16 June 1977. That afternoon, I returned to England for a brief visit to my grandmother before seeking work for the summer. I needed to earn money before starting my university studies for the priesthood.

One of my fellow students in Cork had been Gregory Crowhurst, who had become my closest friend and was someone in whom I could confide anything. His father was a social worker, who was able to arrange jobs for myself and another student, Len de Sousa, with a children's home attached to the Archdiocese of Southwark.

The home, run by mainly Irish nuns, the Poor Servants of the Mother of God, was in Hove, on the coast next to Brighton in East Sussex. We were paid £25 a week plus our room and board.

Len, who was a good-looking Portuguese Indian from Mozambique, turned out to be a great charmer with women and within a week had several different girls in tow. He was incredibly naughty and destined not to last long in a seminary. Years later, he invited me to assist at his wedding.

Several young social workers were attached to the home and with them I enjoyed another happy and pleasurable summer. Alone I used to take out about 20 children at a time, into the town or down to the beach – something I don't think would be allowed today. But the children were by and large well behaved and there was only one occasion when I lost any of them.

They were twins who had wandered off while we were all paddling in the sea and I didn't realise they were missing until I returned to the home. I raced back to the beach in a blind panic, fearing the worst – that they had drowned or been snatched by foreign slave traders. But fortunately I found them straight away, still splashing happily in the shallows and unaware that the rest of us had gone.

On another occasion, I was asked to join two of the nuns, who were taking a party of children to Westminster Cathedral for the annual children's service.

It was there, quite by accident, that I first met the man

who was to have a profound influence on my future vocation almost a decade later – Cardinal Basil Hume.

A year earlier, with remarkable boldness, Basil Hume, a Benedictine monk, had been plucked from relative obscurity as Abbot of Ampleforth in Yorkshire, by Pope Paul VI, and made Archbishop of Westminster. A few weeks later, the Pope raised him to Cardinal.

This incredibly simple and holy man, who was to transform my own life, was to transform the image of Catholicism in Britain, making it more attractive and credible than it had been for decades, even centuries. Before his death in 1999, he would become more deeply loved, by people of all denominations and none, than any other churchman in this or virtually any other country. He was the spiritual leader of the nation.

He found our little group hovering in the main aisle as he returned from saying goodbye to people in the piazza outside the Cathedral. He was alone and on his way to get out of his formal robes.

He stopped and asked where the children were from and then, squatting down to their height, introduced himself to each of them in turn and asked their names.

Then he asked about me and seemed genuinely interested when I told him I had completed my novitiate and was about to start my university course.

'It's been very nice to meet you all,' he said, 'and it would be nice to see you again, and hear how you get on.'

I was to learn that he was always this chatty and didn't use what I call 'holy language'. That wasn't his style.

Later that year, I often used the Cathedral for confession and would sometimes run into him. He had a tremendous memory for people and always remembered who I was and had a few kind words to offer.

Despite my serious misgivings that I was on the wrong vocational track, but not having found an order which better suited my needs, I eventually took my place in the SMA's House of Studies in Barnet, in north London, which was my intended home for the next two years.

I would study for my degree course in philosophy at the Missionary Institute at Mill Hill, which is associated with the Catholic University of Louvain in Belgium. We commuted to the college each day by minibus. There were religious orders there from all over Europe and a dozen nationalities.

My course of study at the college was a serious matter, putting me under pressure to pass important exams for the first time. Fortunately for me, the continental system in use there relied on oral examinations and so I was able to cope with most of my subjects. Greek was the exception in requiring a written test, and here I was out of my league, but, thanks to the Herculean efforts of a private tutor, I managed to scrape through. I briefly touched on Hebrew and Latin and somehow scrambled through those exams as well, successfully emerging from my first year's finals with a pass.

Then it was back to the children's home in Hove to start a summer of work.

By this time, I had become religious-order promiscuous, looking round for new ones the way most young men of my age were looking round for new partners. I stayed at Worth Abbey, near Gatwick, and visited several other religious orders in the south-east during my month in Hove, but found nothing which stimulated a real interest.

Then came a significant breakthrough: a meeting with the Franciscans of the Atonement. Their mission to help the poor and the needy and spread the belief of spiritual unity among the world's religions instantly struck a vibrant chord deep inside me.

The way it came about was as though divine providence was at work again, this time in the shape of a little old lady who lived in Hove.

My duty on that particular Sunday was to take a group of children to Mass, and instead of taking them as usual to the church of St Mary Magdalene, where the sermons were long and boring, I thought, I took them to the Sacred Heart, where the kids could enjoy a lighter service.

After Mass, I was pulled into conversation by Mrs Wynne Monen, who invited me to join her later at her home in Hove for coffee. It transpired that this elderly lady's daughter, Loretta, had worked as a receptionist for a group of Franciscan friars in America, one of whom now lived in London, and came to see her each month. She told me they appeared to be a very nice order and gave me some of their literature.

When I read of their ecumenism and interfaith dialogue and their devotion to the poor and needy, I told her that I would love to meet them. So she wrote to her friend and before long it was arranged that I should go to London and visit their friary in Westminster — the place I now call home.

I had dinner there with the Father Superior in London, Father Alban Carroll. He was the first American I had ever encountered and I found him surprisingly easygoing. He made me feel very welcome. But he also cautioned me, 'Michael, you are the property of the SMA. You belong to them and can't just walk out on them for another order without thinking about it very carefully.'

Which I did, over the next six weeks.

The previous year in Hove I had met an Italian priest who was the head of a school in Spain. He had kept in touch and this year had invited me and a friend to teach English in his school for six weeks. He would pay our costs and for our work with him. And as a bonus I would learn Spanish.

So, after my time in Hove, I set off for Spain with Gregory Crowhurst. We took rucksacks and a tent and sleeping bags and made our way down to Aranjuez — of guitar-concerto fame — south of Madrid.

At the end of six idyllic weeks, I had made up my mind. I would tell the Franciscan friars that I wanted to join them.

This time I was greeted at the London friary by Father

Peter Taran, who had just arrived from America. He was an Italian-American in his early forties, streetwise, full of enthusiasm and spontaneity and big in the renewal of charismatic Catholic-Pentecostal-style worship.

'If God is calling you to us,' he told me, 'then we will take you. The Holy Spirit has led you to us here and that's good enough for us.'

It's a fact that, ever since then, I have loved boring sermons. For, had I not taken the children to the Sacred Heart because of the boring sermons at the Church of Mary Magdalene, I would never have met Mrs Monen and the Franciscans.

At last, I felt I was on the right track and when I returned to Mill Hill that September I immediately sought out my Superior at the SMA and told him my decision.

I gathered it was as much of a relief for him as it was for me. He had known for some time that I wasn't happy with them and he had heard from other students of my visits to different religious orders over the preceding 12 months.

In making the break, I felt that a great burden had been lifted off my shoulders, but I suddenly realised, on a practical level, that I was now in a no man's land of my own making. I didn't belong to anyone. At that stage, I was an aspirant for the Franciscans but not even an official candidate. I had nowhere to live and how could I stay in college if I was no longer a student for the priesthood?

The SMA were marvellous. At no cost, they allowed me to continue my degree course as a lay student, the first ever in the college's history, and a monk. Dom Edmund Jones OSB, who had been my sometime confessor, arranged a room at his monastery in Cockfosters, not far from the college, in exchange for cleaning and household duties.

I was even invited to drop in for breakfast with my old room-mates in Barnet and travel to college in their minibus. They proved to be true friends and I am still in touch with some of them today, including the present head of the SMA, who had been a classmate of mine in Cork.

The next significant occurence came in April 1979, when I found myself on a Freddie Laker flight to New York and my beckoning new life as a Franciscan friar.

I was met at the airport by two friars, who drove me for two hours along the Hudson River to Garrison, where the highest mountain in the valley reared up before us. At its peak loomed a truly enormous monastery, a vast eight-storey structure of concrete and glass, almost a quarter of a mile in length.

It looked cold and uninviting like something out of Russia during the Cold War, a veritable *Titanic* of a building stranded on top of the mountain. This was Graymoor, home of the Franciscans of the Atonement.

Surrounding it was a brilliant area of breathtaking natural beauty, like the best of Scotland and Wales combined – a definite candidate for the eighth wonder of the world.

Beyond the monastic monstrosity was the original friary and church, with an Italianate tower, built around 1910 and simply and beautifully crafted in wood and stone.

The gardens at Graymoor covered hundreds of acres and were laid out like a religious Disneyland. There you could do the Stations of the Cross and visit the site of Calvary and the grotto at Lourdes, among many other devotional shrines.

At that time, up to 20,000 pilgrims a day visited the monastery and its gardens at peak times of the year. There was even a huge children's fairground where the kids could play while adults toured the grounds.

Halfway down the mountain was St Christopher's Inn, named after the patron saint of travellers and dedicated to the homeless and needy, which it served. The Inn had been started soon after the founder, Father Paul Wattson, arrived at Graymoor in 1898, and originally had one homeless man living in a chicken coop. It grew to become the biggest centre for the homeless and needy in the United States.

Father Wattson chose the name 'Franciscan Friars of the Atonement' because atonement in the Bible means the unity of men and women with God and one another. Their mission was to serve the poor, the needy and the homeless, those in hospitals and prisons and people recovering from alcoholism and chemical dependency, and, through their ecumenical ministries, to bring people of the various Christian churches and other world religions closer together.

The small group of Atonement Friars and Atonement Sisters under Father Paul and his co-founder, Mother Lurana White, were received into the Catholic Church in 1909, under Pope Pius X, and encouraged to continue their work for Christian unity.

Today, the Friars of the Atonement serve as ecumenical officers in dioceses in the United Sates, Canada, England and Japan, furthering the founders' belief in Jesus' prayer: 'That all may be one so that the world might believe.'

The friars at Graymoor seemed to seek and bring out the best in one another and I was immediately adopted by the community. Even more than my experience with the Crowhurst family, I had finally found a place where I was in harmony with the people around me and my surroundings, and I knew that I had reached my spiritual home at last.

But there was still much work to be done.

Within days, I was introduced to Dan Callahan from Buffalo, New York, and we spoke together on the telephone with Jim Lindsay in Philadelphia. We had been told that the three of us were to enter the order's friary, or House of Studies, at the Catholic University in Washington DC, as postulants. That is, as candidates for admission into the order who were not yet novices.

But that was still a whole year away. First I must return to England and complete my degree course. Those final months seemed to fly past and suddenly it was September, and my finals were over The Franciscans may have accepted me as a candidate, but I would not begin my studies in America until the following May. And until then I needed to find a job.

Luckily, Gregory Crowhurst's father came to the rescue again and found me a job in a children's home in Bexhill-on-Sea in East Sussex. I worked there until Christmas. I was bored but happy enough and the tedium was reduced by visits from Father Peter and my occasional weekend trips to see him in the Westminster friary.

In January, the Crowhursts invited me to move in with them and become part of the family. By then, Gregory had also left the SMA and was studying to become a social worker like his father.

He had a brother Michael, a great guy who was wild and a hippy, and a smashing sister called Hilary. I became like a brother to the three of them and suddenly found the secure happy family I had always longed for.

During the day, I had the unlikely job of making pallets in a factory at Erith in Kent, and by the start of April I had saved enough to be able to take a short holiday before leaving for America. Once again, Gregory and I dug out our rucksacks and camping gear and headed for Holland, where we stayed in a campsite just outside Amsterdam.

It was a holiday of sharp contrasts. We walked around the red-light district and saw the ladies sitting in their windows advertising their services and offering their wares, and Gregory took me to a couple of very risqué movies. But we also went to the house of Anne Frank, which was a very moving experience, and visited The Hague.

In April I was again on my way to America, and in May Dan Callahan, Jim Lidsay and I gathered at Graymoor and drove down to the New Jersey turnpike all the way from New York to Washington.

The Washington Friary consisted of we three postulants, no novices, five students in simple vows and eight friars who were in life vows, some ordained priests and some brothers who were not ordained.

There was also a Guardian, as in guardian angel, in overall charge of the Friary, who in other orders would normally have the title 'Superior', a Novice Master and a Postulant Master, Father Adrian, plus an administrator and several friar priests doing advanced studies at the Catholic University of America (CUA).

The Friary, which was to be my home for the next four and a half years, was on the University's campus, where, dotted around, were various houses of religious orders – Jesuits, Carmelites, Franciscans, Dominicans, Marists and others. The University was famous not only for its Department of Religious Studies but also for medicine, drama and law.

We spent our first six months in prayer and meditation and studying theology and were declared ready for the clothing ceremony. For this, we were returned to Graymoor, where the order's Superior General helped us, for the first time, into our friar's brown habits, which symbolised the beginning of our year as novices. These habits were tied around the waist with the traditional white cords of the Franciscans.

It was to be a year spent in the Washington Friary, an oasis year during which we partly withdrew from the world and devoted our time to prayer and spiritual study. This led, in January 1982, to our making our first vows.

As newly professed friars, the three of us, Dan, Jim and myself, began a six-month pre-theology course at the Washington Theological Union at Silver Spring in Maryland, across the state line but just a mile and a half from the Friary.

We studied Canon, or Church, law, spirituality, theology and liturgy: the rituals of the Church.

During this period, I made contact with the Dean of Theology at the University, Father John Ford, and gave him all my certificates and results which I had received from the Missionary Institute at Mill Hill, which was, like CUA, a Pontifical University. He checked with the Institute and eventually told me that he could accept my Bachelor of Philosophy degree study in England as being on a level with its American equivalent, and that it was therefore sufficient to gain me entry to the Master of Divinity course, starting in September 1982, for which the Franciscans had enrolled me.

Had they not recognised my English degree, it would

have meant starting all over again from scratch. I am not absolutely certain I could have coped with such a mammoth setback. Thank goodness I was never put to the test.

But, before coming to grips with my Master's Degree I had the summer to get through and a more practical assignment thrown at me. I was sent back to England for three months to gain practical experience in a really needy parish in Thornton Heath in south London. St Andrew's Church tragically achieved some notoriety a few years later when a man with a sabre ran amok, hacking at members of the congregation. It was my first taste of working in a real parish and I became very involved in the lives of its parishioners.

Father Jim Hurley was an example of the priesthood at its very best, compassionate, helpful and caring, but strong and commanding when needed. The ideal combination to cope with such a tough parish.

There were many lovely people there, but they had many problems to cope with: domestic, financial, criminal and racial issues, against a background of friction between the black, Asian and white communities. I loved it, and a few years later after I was ordained a priest, I went back there to celebrate one of my first masses with the great Father Hurley.

This was also the year of the first-ever papal visit to Britain, and the Franciscan magazine *Ecumenical Trends* asked me to cover the Pope's visit and write an article on its ecumenical aspects. For this task, I was given a press pass and was one of a small media group who were privileged to shake the Pope's hand when he visited Westminster Cathedral, little dreaming that I would be working in that same Cathedral just two and a half years hence.

Another highlight was being invited to have lunch with Cardinal Hume, who still remembered me and wanted to know all about my adventures in America.

That summer flew past and after a brief visit to my grandmother, and an even briefer visit to my Aunt Sheila in Halewood, who was now alone after the death of her mother, I returned to America.

I had long before decided to make peace with Aunt Sheila and she seemed immensely happy that I had taken the trouble to visit her. I came away pleased to have faced and dismissed one of the horrors of my childhood, my time in Grandma Seed's house, and inordinately happy that Aunt Sheila should have reacted so warmly. To my great delight, she had even asked me to call her Sheila.

That September, I was introduced to two of the world's greatest theologians.

My professor of theology was Father, in 2001 to become Cardinal, Avery Dulles, the Jesuit son of former Secretary of State John Foster Dulles. His uncles were head of the FBI and the Attorney General. A powerful political clan similar in many ways to the Kennedys.

Father Avery could not have been kinder to me. He

was a very practical as well as a very holy man and became a kind of academic tutor to me in my years at the Catholic University.

For moral theology, I had Father Charles Curran, who since the 1960s had been under investigation by the Holy See, the Vatican, for excessive liberalism. Towards the end of the decade, when the Vatican first tried to remove him, the whole of the University had gone on strike until the threat was withdrawn. He was immensely popular with his students and deeply respected by them all as a remarkable human being and an outstanding Christian.

He was still being investigated during my time there and I must say it was very interesting to have him as my teacher of moral theology.

There was one other professor there, a nun called Sister Elizabeth Johnson, who was also a famous American theologian. But we had a difference of opinion when she decided she wanted me to drop my degree course. It all came about because of the old problem from my childhood: my inability to cope with written exams under pressure.

My first exams at the Catholic University were a rerun of my 11-plus. I left all my exam papers blank.

Fathers Dulles and Curran were curious and called me in to discuss it. After hearing my story, they said that, if the problem was a genuine one, they would be happy to test me orally.

They agreed it was best if they sent me to the School

for Educational Learning, there at CUA, and see if there was evidence to back up my story.

'We have no problem giving you oral exams, none at all, and we will. But, for your sake and ours, let's find out exactly what the problem is. So would you mind being analysed and assessed by top educationalists at the school? You will probably be helping their research studies at the same time.'

The outcome was that the experts concluded I was seriously dyslexic and, though I had somehow learned to read well, after all their tests agreed I was incapable of producing the written word under pressure.

In reflective mood I could write. But under stress, no.

They believed that, because of a childhood devoid of education and never being called on to do traditional exams, the written test was not a good format for me. In speech, on the other hand, I was excellent and had an exceptional memory. It was a fantastic report and Fathers Dulles and Curran accepted its recommendations without hesitation.

From then on, my exam results were superb. They would ask questions and it was difficult to stop me talking. I was like a computer. Until the end of my course, my results were very good.

But it was a very different story with Sister Elizabeth. The blank sheet had been of concern to her. Her reaction was rigidly traditional.

'If you can't express yourself on paper, I don't think you'll be able to fulfil this course,' she told me. 'Perhaps you should consider not becoming a priest but remaining a friar brother.'

What she meant was that I should not become an ordained friar. I pointed that out to her and told her that Religious brothers were the intellectual equal of Religious priests. St Francis himself was not a priest.

'Just because I can't pass written exams doesn't mean I can't pass exams at all,' I told her.

But she refused to change her mind, even after being told that Fathers Dulles and Curran, the two greats, had agreed to examine me orally. She failed me. So I left her class and found another lecturer to cover the same ground who would give me oral tests. I passed everything with top marks.

Sister Elizabeth was what priests in America describe as a 'free-range nun'. They have a quaint way of differentiating between modern and traditionally dressed nuns. Those who still wear the full veils and headgear and robes are referred to as 'battery nuns'. 'Free-range nuns' wear modern clothes and look like executives. It is not meant in a hurtful way but as a light-hearted way of describing the marked differences between different orders of nuns in today's world.

That summer, for my practical experience I was sent to Los Angeles and made a chaplain attached to the Hollywood Presbyterian Hospital. It was in a really violent area full of shootings, stabbings, rape and violence – and I loved every moment of it. This was real life and real emotion and like being a character in a *Kojak* movie.

I lived in a small friary not far from the hospital and was given a huge old car to drive back and forth. I visited all the patients of any and every creed. Catholics, Protestants, Jews and Muslims all got a visit from Brother Michael. There seemed to be every type there, from Hollywood producers and actors to gangsters and policemen with gunshot wounds.

It was there that I conducted my first funeral, a tragic event involving a young actor. On a happier note, I also managed a day trip to Las Vegas and won a few dollars on the slot machines in Caesar's Palace, and drove up the coast to San Francisco, one of the nicest cities I have ever visited. I travelled with Father Art Johnson, who was to become our Superior General.

It was a fabulous two months, a mixture of glamour and despair, and I learned a great deal about ministering to the needy and the sick and about the tarnished side of Tinseltown and its amazingly varied inhabitants. It was a rich and rewarding learning experience.

The following summer, after another year's study in Washington, I was sent, in contrast, to our own St Christopher's Inn at Graymoor. There were several hundred homeless and needy people staying there at the time, mainly from New York. Some were itinerant down-and-outs, others newly homeless and many were either drug addicts or alcoholics.

I helped in the clothing centre, the kitchens and in the

detox centre, talking with them, encouraging them to stick to their programmes of recovery and trying to instil hope in them. It was often harrowing work, but great experience for the future. Eighteen months later, I celebrated my first mass in the Inn chapel.

Three different summers and three vastly different experiences: the tough London parish, the bustling hospital set in an area of desperate poverty and violence, and our own centre for the homeless with its heartbreaking quota of broken and hopeless cases. Each experience had helped to develop within me the compassion and the instinct and the intuition I would need to be truly helpful to others and make a genuine difference in people's lives – God willing.

At the end of my time with St Christopher's Inn, I was allowed a short break in England and was again invited to have lunch with Cardinal Hume.

The friars had already decided that I should be sent to Westminster Cathedral after taking my final vows, and become a deacon there. The Cardinal had told them that he would be pleased to accept me as he already knew me.

I sensed then that this holy and humble man, with such a lively sense of fun and serenity, could one day become a good friend, and I marvelled at my great good fortune.

That November, I completed my Master's Degree in Divinity, at a good level, and on 6 January, the Feast of Epiphany, I made my final vows at Graymoor.

Four days later, I was on my way to London, accompanied by my old friend Father Peter Taran, who had become Vicar General of my order, the second in command. He was with me to attend my ordination, as a deacon at Westminster Cathedral on 19 January 1985. It was performed by the Bishop of Leeds, William Gordon Wheeler, who was the founder of my order in England and had become a kind of uncle to me over the years.

A deacon can do the same things as a priest with the exception of celebrating Mass, hearing confessions and anointing the sick. One of my jobs was to assist the Cardinal at all the big ceremonies in the Cathedral and elsewhere, and walk in front of him, which developed our friendship.

The following January I returned to Graymoor to be ordained a priest by Bishop Eugene Marino. We had become very good friends in Washington and I had asked him whether, if I ever made it, he would come to Graymoor to ordain me.

He flew up from Washington especially to officiate at my ordination on the 18th. Eugene Marino later became Archbishop of Atlanta, Georgia, and the first black archbishop in America. Sadly, he was forced to resign in 1990 after becoming involved in a scandalous affair with a woman.

I was told by the friars that I would spend a further period at Westminster Cathedral and then be reassigned elsewhere.

But Cardinal Hume had other ideas, and on 1 January 1988, when I was due to return to America for reassignment, he asked me if I would become his Secretary for Ecumenical Affairs and the Superior General agreed. I accepted with joy and gratitude and began an eventful and extremely happy 11-year association with him which I still cherish.

I was even more delighted when his successor, Cardinal Cormac Murphy-O'Connor, asked me in the spring of 2000 if I would continue in that role during his tenure as archbishop – a ministry I still hold to this day.

Since the hardback version of this book appeared a wonderful thing has happened. My real mother, Marie, read my story and has made contact. We have met and I was introduced to the stepsister and brother I never knew I had, Lisa who is 39 and George who is 36.

We are still in the process of getting to know one another but to have found my lost family is one of the most joyful experiences of my life. It is still a bit strange for everyone, as until very recently Lisa and George had no idea that I existed. There is so much we all want to learn about one another and we accept that this could take years. But the mere fact that we have met, and are talking, is a minor miracle for me. To be held and kissed by my real mother is a wondrous thing that I never, in my wildest imaginings, believed could happen.

Marie, my mother, now lives alone in the Midlands. Her children live nearby. She told me that it was in

Manchester that I was conceived. She was only sixteen when she met my father, Steven, who was also sixteen, in the autumn of 1956. He had travelled from Oxfordshire to Manchester with his parents, who were visiting family, and met my mother at a local dance. 'It was love at first sight', she told me. But their whirlwind romance never stood a chance of ending in any way other than badly. 'We were so young and so foolish, we just couldn't help ourselves. But after a few days he was gone and I never heard from him again', she said. 'After you were born I looked after you for as long as I could, until, eventually, I was unable to cope. I found it so hard to let go and even after I had handed you over to the Catholic children's home I went there every day to see you and hold you. Until the day I was told I wasn't allowed to be with you any more. Your adoptive parents had come to get you. I was permitted to watch the three of you together through an observation window. They were well dressed and looked very respectable. Like very fine people. Little did we know what would unfold.'